The definitive
management ideas
of the year from
Harvard Business Review.

2023

RCP-
1854

definitive collection of ideas
experienced leaders alike.
g selected from the pages of
critical to the success of

HBR's 10 Must Reads 2017
HBR's 10 Must Reads 2018
HBR's 10 Must Reads 2019
HBR's 10 Must Reads 2020
HBR's 10 Must Reads 2021
HBR's 10 Must Reads 2022
HBR's 10 Must Reads for CEOs
HBR's 10 Must Reads for New Managers
HBR's 10 Must Reads on AI, Analytics, and the New Machine Age
HBR's 10 Must Reads on Boards
HBR's 10 Must Reads on Building a Great Culture
HBR's 10 Must Reads on Business Model Innovation
HBR's 10 Must Reads on Career Resilience
HBR's 10 Must Reads on Change Management (Volumes 1 and 2)
HBR's 10 Must Reads on Collaboration
HBR's 10 Must Reads on Communication (Volumes 1 and 2)
HBR's 10 Must Reads on Creativity
HBR's 10 Must Reads on Design Thinking
HBR's 10 Must Reads on Diversity
HBR's 10 Must Reads on Emotional Intelligence
HBR's 10 Must Reads on Entrepreneurship and Startups
HBR's 10 Must Reads on High Performance
HBR's 10 Must Reads on Innovation
HBR's 10 Must Reads on Leadership (Volumes 1 and 2)
HBR's 10 Must Reads on Leadership for Healthcare

HBR's 10 Must Reads on Leadership Lessons from Sports
HBR's 10 Must Reads on Leading Digital Transformation
HBR's 10 Must Reads on Lifelong Learning
HBR's 10 Must Reads on Making Smart Decisions
HBR's 10 Must Reads on Managing Across Cultures
HBR's 10 Must Reads on Managing in a Downturn, Expanded Edition
HBR's 10 Must Reads on Managing People (Volumes 1 and 2)
HBR's 10 Must Reads on Managing Risk
HBR's 10 Must Reads on Managing Yourself (Volumes 1 and 2)
HBR's 10 Must Reads on Mental Toughness
HBR's 10 Must Reads on Negotiation
HBR's 10 Must Reads on Nonprofits and the Social Sectors
HBR's 10 Must Reads on Organizational Resilience
HBR's 10 Must Reads on Platforms and Ecosystems
HBR's 10 Must Reads on Public Speaking and Presenting
HBR's 10 Must Reads on Reinventing HR
HBR's 10 Must Reads on Sales
HBR's 10 Must Reads on Strategic Marketing
HBR's 10 Must Reads on Strategy (Volumes 1 and 2)
HBR's 10 Must Reads on Strategy for Healthcare
HBR's 10 Must Reads on Teams
HBR's 10 Must Reads on Women and Leadership
HBR's 10 Must Reads: The Essentials

HBR'S 10 MUST READS

The definitive
management ideas
of the year from
Harvard Business Review.

2023

HARVARD BUSINESS REVIEW PRESS
Boston, Massachusetts

The web addresses referenced in this book were live and correct at the time of the book's publication but may be subject to change.

Library of Congress Cataloging-in-Publication Data

Names: Harvard Business Review Press, editor.
   Title: HBR's 10 must reads 2023 / Harvard Business Review.
   Other titles: Harvard Business Review's ten must reads 2023 |
      HBR's 10 must reads (Series)
   Description: Boston, Massachusetts : Harvard Business Review Press, [2022] |
      Series: HBR's 10 must reads | Includes index. |
   Identifiers: LCCN 2022021140 (print) | LCCN 2022021141 (ebook) |
      ISBN 9781647824556 (paperback) | ISBN 9781647824563 (epub)
   Subjects: LCSH: Success in business. | Industrial management.
   Classification: LCC HF5386 .H34845 2022 (print) | LCC HF5386 (ebook) |
      DDC 650.1—dc23/eng/20220603
   LC record available at https://lccn.loc.gov/2022021140
   LC ebook record available at https://lccn.loc.gov/2022021141

ISBN: 978-1-64782-213-2
eISBN: 978-1-64782-214-9

The paper used in this publication meets the requirements of the American National Standard for Permanence of Paper for Publications and Documents in Libraries and Archives Z39.48-1992.

Contents

Editors' Note   ix

The Future of Flexibility at Work   1
by Ellen Ernst Kossek, Patricia Gettings, and Kaumudi Misra

Eliminate Strategic Overload   37
by Felix Oberholzer-Gee

Drive Innovation with Better Decision-Making   53
by Linda A. Hill, Emily Tedards, and Taran Swan

Unconscious Bias Training That Works   67
by Francesca Gino and Katherine Coffman

Why You Aren't Getting More from Your Marketing AI   83
by Eva Ascarza, Michael Ross, and Bruce G. S. Hardie

Net Promoter 3.0   93
by Fred Reichheld, Darci Darnell, and Maureen Burns

How Chinese Retailers Are Reinventing
the Customer Journey   107
by Mark J. Greeven, Katherine Xin, and George S. Yip

The Circular Business Model   121
by Atalay Atasu, Céline Dumas, and Luk N. Van Wassenhove

How to Succeed Quickly in a New Role   135
by Rob Cross, Greg Pryor, and David Sylvester

Accounting for Climate Change   147
by Robert S. Kaplan and Karthik Ramanna

BONUS ARTICLE
Persuading the Unpersuadable   165
   by Adam Grant

About the Contributors   173
Index   177

Editors' Note

When our editorial team met—some members on-screen, and some gathered around a conference table—to discuss the past year's issues of *Harvard Business Review*, we were still adjusting to what we could only assume was the new normal. During the past few years many organizations were in reactive mode, shifting how they worked as the changing environment—and the Covid-19 pandemic—dictated, for reasons of safety or out of a sense of urgency. But now leaders, managers, and individuals alike have an opportunity to define a different path, not by reacting to the present but by creating a new future. The 11 articles we've selected for this volume reflect that.

Organizations are experimenting with and adopting flexible work practices that increase employee engagement, retention, and satisfaction, and reassessing their strategies to create greater value for customers, employees, and suppliers. In this volume we see that employees want to get up to speed faster in new roles, not just for their own sake but for the betterment of their organizations and networks. We look across geographic borders to learn how new technologies can create better customer experiences. We reevaluate two established practices—the Net Promoter System and unconscious bias training—to make them applicable in a more purposeful and equitable future. And as pressure grows to fight greenhouse gas emissions and create sustainable—and efficient—supply chains, we spotlight new accounting practices to hold corporations to high standards and rethink product life cycles.

We start with **"The Future of Flexibility at Work,"** which asks, "What does flexibility at work look like in practice?" Most organizations approach it in one of two ways: as an ad hoc work-life accommodation available on request, or as giving people permission to get their work done on their own schedule—as long as they're available 24/7 to answer emails or put out fires. Neither approach is sustainable over the long term. Ellen Ernst Kossek, Patricia Gettings, and Kaumudi Misra, researchers who have been studying workplace flexibility for years, advocate an approach to more equally balance employer and employee needs. In this article they outline the tenets that organizations should follow as they develop their own flexible programs and policies.

At any given time your company is focused on more than a handful of strategies at once— marketing, social, and global, among many others—but companies have little to show for an uptick in initiatives. In **"Eliminate Strategic Overload,"** Felix Oberholzer-Gee argues that managers face an attractive, back-to-basics opportunity. He explains that a strategic initiative is worthwhile only if it creates value for customers, employees, or suppliers. And as companies increase the total amount of value created, they position themselves for enduring financial success. Oberholzer-Gee offers advice on how to select fewer initiatives with greater impact so that companies can make their strategies more powerful.

One area that often derails strategy execution is innovation. In **"Drive Innovation with Better Decision-Making,"** Linda A. Hill, Emily Tedards, and Taran Swan declare that today's discovery-driven innovation processes are an outdated, inefficient approach to decision-making. Those processes involve an unprecedented number of choices, leading to slow decisions that are informed by obsolete information and narrow perspectives. Drawing on the transformation at Pfizer's Global Clinical Supply, which went on to play a critical role in supporting the rapid development of the pharma giant's Covid-19 vaccine, the authors explain how organizations can apply agile and lean principles to decision-making to make rapid experimentation pay off.

Becoming more diverse, equitable, and inclusive has become a common goal in organizations, and to live up to that objective, many companies have turned to unconscious bias (UB) training. But according to research by Francesca Gino and Katherine Coffman, most UB training is ineffective. To get results, it must teach attendees to manage their biases, practice new behaviors, and track their progress. What's more, proper training entails a long journey and structural organizational changes. In **"Unconscious Bias Training That Works,"** Gino and Coffman use examples from Microsoft and Starbucks to offer advice on implementing a rigorous UB program that will help employees overcome denial and act on their awareness, develop the empathy that combats bias, diversify their networks, and commit to improvement.

Fewer than 40% of companies that invest in AI see gains from it, usually owing to one or more of these errors: They ask the wrong questions, leading AI to solve the wrong problem. They assume that all prediction mistakes are equivalent, not seeing the difference between the value of being right and the costs of being wrong. Or they stick with outdated practices and don't leverage AI's ability to make far more frequent and granular decisions. In **"Why You Aren't Getting More from Your Marketing AI,"** Eva Ascarza, Michael Ross, and Bruce G. S. Hardie suggest ways for marketers and data science teams to communicate better among themselves and to avoid those pitfalls, getting much higher returns on their AI efforts.

Since its introduction, in 2003, the Net Promoter System, which measures how consistently brands turn customers into advocates, has become the predominant customer success framework. But as its popularity grew, NPS was gamed and misused in ways that hurt its credibility. Over time its creator, Fred Reichheld, realized that the only way to correct that problem was to introduce a hard, complementary metric that would draw on accounting results. In **"Net Promoter 3.0,"** Reichheld, Darci Darnell, and Maureen Burns introduce the *earned growth rate,* which captures the revenue generated by returning customers and their referrals. This article teaches readers how to track metrics that help companies validate investments in customer service and convince investors of their businesses' underlying strength.

In addition to focusing on earned growth rates, organizations should prioritize tracking customer data. In **"How Chinese Retailers Are Reinventing the Customer Journey,"** Mark J. Greeven, Katherine Xin, and George S. Yip explain why Western retailers trail their Chinese counterparts in leveraging customer data to make better business decisions, increase operational efficiency, and reduce costs. From their research on Chinese retailers the authors have drawn five lessons that Western companies can learn from China as they develop their own digital market offerings: create single entry points, embed digital evaluation in the customer journey, don't think of sales as isolated events, rethink the logistical fundamentals, and always stay close to the customer.

More and more manufacturing companies are talking about what's often called the circular economy—in which businesses can create supply chains that recover or recycle the resources used to create their products. But creating a circular business model is challenging, and taking the wrong approach can be expensive. Drawing on decades of research, Atalay Atasu, Céline Dumas, and Luk N. Van Wassenhove argue in **"The Circular Business Model"** that success depends on many factors, but perhaps the most important is choosing a strategy that aligns with a company's capabilities and resources—while addressing the constraints on its operations. The authors identify three basic strategies for achieving circularity and offer a tool to help manufacturers identify which is most likely to be economically sustainable.

"How to Succeed Quickly in a New Role" speaks to the millions of individuals who have embarked on a role transition this past year. Whether it's a promotion, a move to another organization, or a strategic new challenge in a different department, this professional shift can be an opportunity to develop yourself and progress in your career. But in today's dynamic workplaces, successful moves aren't as easy as they once were. After analyzing employee relationships and communication patterns across more than 100 companies and interviewing 160 executives in 20 of them, Rob Cross, Greg Pryor, and David Sylvester discovered an overlooked prerequisite for transition success: the effective use of internal networks. In this article they elaborate on five practices that will help those in changing roles get up to speed faster.

Corporations face growing pressure—from investors, advocacy groups, politicians, and even business leaders themselves—to reduce greenhouse gas (GHG) emissions from their operations and their supply and distribution chains. About 90% of the companies in the S&P 500 now issue some form of environmental, social, and governance report, which almost always includes an estimate of the company's GHG emissions. Robert S. Kaplan and Karthik Ramanna describe these as "catchall reports that are often made up of inaccurate, unverifiable, and contradictory data." They propose a remedy: the *E-liability accounting system,* whereby emissions are measured using a combination of chemistry and engineering, and principles of cost accounting are applied to assign the emissions to individual outputs. **"Accounting for Climate Change"** provides a detailed method for assigning E-liabilities across your entire value chain.

We close this book with **"Persuading the Unpersuadable,"** by Adam Grant. Many of us may be asking ourselves how, when people discount our views, we can persuade them to rethink their positions. Grant writes, "It is possible to get even the most overconfident, stubborn, narcissistic, and disagreeable people to open their minds." An organizational psychologist, he has spent time with people who succeeded in motivating the notoriously self-confident Steve Jobs to change his mind and has analyzed the science behind their techniques. He offers approaches that can help you encourage a know-it-all to recognize when there's something to be learned, a stubborn colleague to make a U-turn, a narcissist to show humility, and an argumentative boss to agree with you.

As you read through this collection, we hope you feel inspired to rethink your processes, assumptions, strategies, and priorities—not out of necessity but as an opportunity to shape the future you want and to move forward quickly and efficiently.

—The Editors

HBR'S 10 MUST READS

The definitive
management ideas
of the year from
Harvard Business Review.

2023

The Future of Flexibility at Work

by Ellen Ernst Kossek, Patricia Gettings, and Kaumudi Misra

AS ORGANIZATIONS TENTATIVELY PLAN HOW to get work done amid the uncertainty of the coronavirus, both leaders and employees are touting the benefits of flexibility. But what does flexibility at work look like in practice? And how can you know whether your team or organization is using it successfully?

We are researchers who study how organizations of all types—from professional services and IT firms to hospitals, retail stores, and manufacturing facilities—manage flexibility. Over the course of our work we have asked leaders to tell us how they do so (or not). Here is a range of typical responses:

I accommodate employee needs for time to go to the gym during lunch or take a class by allowing a special arrangement with respect to the work schedule.

If a family member is ill or someone has been in a car accident, it's no issue to leave work.

Because of the way that the units are staffed and scheduled, there doesn't seem to be a whole lot of flexibility.

I often resorted to mandatory Zoom meetings on Friday nights at 6 p.m. because that was the only calendar opening for key staff members.

We can't get enough staff on the weekends to run the production we need to run—even with eight different schedule options. That's not a good thing. I don't want that to be the reason we can't produce.

These responses may sound familiar. The variation among them is notable. The first focuses on special arrangements for nonwork activities. The second is contingent on dire circumstances. The third expresses frustration about the barriers to flexibility. The fourth is flexibility at its worst. The last shows that flexible scheduling is a critical (yet unsolved) competitive issue for many organizations.

This variation reflects the fact that the word *flexibility* is vague; its implementation can differ from organization to organization, department to department, and even within teams. It's no wonder that managers struggle with how to let employees work when and where they do so best. Even companies that were early leaders in piloting extensive flexible working—such as IBM and Bank of America—began pulling back on those arrangements several years ago, because they felt their businesses weren't benefiting.

Yet coming out of the pandemic, a growing number of companies have announced that they plan to "embrace flexibility," particularly in a hybrid working model. This is for three key reasons: First, businesses believe that the 24/7 remote-work form of flexibility can be leveraged to support productivity. Second, employees—especially Millennials—are threatening to quit unless they're granted flexibility. Third, some leaders assume that when employees are permitted to work flexibly, they automatically experience more harmony in their work-life balance.

But these rationales oversimplify the challenge in making flexibility core to an organization's strategy and operations. As a result, most companies approach the task superficially. In reality, expanding flexible work arrangements entails more than sharing online tool kits, surveying workers' preferences, purchasing self-scheduling software, or hiring consultants to become more "phygital" (physical plus digital). Despite all the hype about flexibility's work-life benefits, studies consistently show that companies are better at creating flexible work options than at enabling the use of them. Leaders leave that to the benefits department or payroll consultants.

Employers also have strong biases regarding the types of flexibility. Research shows that if leaders believe that employees are

Idea in Brief

What does true flexibility look like? Most organizations approach it in one of two ways: as an ad hoc work-life accommodation available upon request, or as giving people permission to get their work done on their own schedule—as long as they're available to answer emails or put out fires 24/7. Neither approach is sustainable over the long term. Authors Ellen Ernst Kossek, Patricia Gettings, and Kaumudi Misra, who have been studying workplace flexibility for years, advocate for a more balanced approach that makes employer and employee needs equal. In this article they outline the downsides of work-life accommodation and boundaryless working, and offer tenets that organizations should follow as they develop their own flexibility programs and policies:

- Make flexibility available to all employees.

- Prioritize clear structures and policies.

- Empower employees to create and manage their own flexibility.

- Remove disincentives for use.

- Remember that you need support from the top.

- Experiment and measure outcomes, including equity.

- Consider the impact of flexibility on your global workforce.

- Remember that implementing flexibility involves a learning curve.

telecommuting to increase productivity, such as by working long hours to meet job demands, then career benefits are likely to ensue. Those benefits are far less prevalent when individuals use flexibility for family or personal reasons. Evidence indicates that when women use flexibility more than men do, they face lower pay, stalled careers, and backlash.

Our worry is that these patterns will recur as organizations plow ahead with flexibility on a much larger scale. But there is a better way. In this article we provide insights on why traditional flexible working practices have not lived up to their potential. We also offer a path forward with what we call *true flexibility*—a strategy that aligns the interests of employers and employees and thus benefits both groups.

The Big Idea: Rethinking "Back to Work"

"THE FUTURE OF FLEXIBILITY AT WORK" is the lead article of **HBR's The Big Idea: Rethinking "Back to Work."** You can read the rest of the series at www.hbr.org/flexibility:

- "12 Questions About Hybrid Work, Answered," by Tsedal Neeley
- "A Guide to Implementing the Four-Day Workweek," by Ashley Whillans and Charlotte Lockhart
- "The Problem with 'Greedy Work,'" by Gretchen Gavett
- "'Remote Work Isn't a Perk to Toss into the Mix,'" by Gretchen Gavett

Traditional Approaches

Leaders have typically managed flexibility in one of two ways: as an *accommodation* around individual work-life events such as illness or childcare, which companies use to attract and retain employees; or as *boundaryless working,* which many leaders used to transition their organizations to widespread remote work during Covid-19. In the second case, employees are expected, explicitly or implicitly, to be available 24/7 to perform their jobs. Whereas accommodation largely offers flexibility for the individual, boundaryless working offers flexibility for the company. Neither is inherently bad, but both can have unintended consequences, particularly when used in isolation.

Accommodation

This approach is understood as a supervisor's one-off response to an employee's request for more flexibility in a schedule, place of work, time off, or workload to support personal or family needs. Such idiosyncratic, case-by-case approvals sometimes mirror parent-child dynamics, with the manager granting "permission" to the employee—whether it's "exceptional flex," as in the hypothetical car accident mentioned above, or a special reward to help retain a high performer.

Benefits can be derived from addressing unique worker needs, but that kind of flexibility may come at a cost if it creates two classes

4

of employees: those who work "nontraditional" schedules and those who work "regular" hours. The latter rarely ask for flexibility but may well want more of it.

Further, many employers have trouble deciding—or are ambivalent about—whether and how to sustain flexible working accommodations, which are rarely implemented in ways that support cultural consistency or career advancement. In organizations where managers are the gatekeepers of flexibility (most often the case), employee access can be very uneven, with accommodation dependent on who one's boss is rather than on the quality of one's work or the equitable support of nonwork needs.

If work flexibility is viewed as an exceptional accommodation, it can also affect customers and clients. In one large North American study, a manager who had supported implementing flexible work commented, "Some clients are more (or less) empathetic than others. . . . You know: 'I'm not paying [the company] to help your people have a nice workload. I need our work done.'"

Finally, we know that women—especially working mothers and caregivers—have historically been the primary seekers of accommodation and have faced pay and career discrimination as a result. Although a smaller number of men seek similar arrangements and may also face discrimination, they are more likely to advance in their careers. Work-life flexibility has long been gender-siloed, seen as a "women's issue," with women bearing the brunt of its effects on career and pay across occupations. This was especially true during the pandemic. For example, the publishing output and productivity of talented STEM professional women decreased dramatically while women handled most of the childcare, eldercare, and schooling.

Boundaryless working

We find that as a company becomes more comfortable with allowing and managing flexibility, leaders tend to move to a boundaryless approach, whereby employees work anywhere, anytime. Typically companies initiate this to enhance productivity and enable their businesses to operate efficiently around the clock while saving money. In the 1990s many companies, including IBM, Deloitte, and

PwC, experimented with this approach, dispersing a mobile workforce globally across home office and customer locations. Leaders learned how to manage performance by relying more on outcome metrics than on face time.

This results-oriented, employer-driven flexibility does indeed yield bottom-line benefits. Studies show that teleworking professionals who are conscientious and highly identified with their jobs are motivated to work long hours, especially in the absence of commutes and watercooler chitchat. And the costs saved from reducing office space are a plus for employers. Yet boundaryless work can hurt employers in the long run, even if they don't realize it. Companies' talent pools may suffer. For example, recent news reports indicate that despite highly lucrative pay, investment banking jobs are now less popular with young professionals because of the long hours, lack of work-life balance, and work-anytime culture.

And although telework provides some benefits to employees, such as a shorter (or no) commute and the ability to integrate home tasks, the evidence suggests a lot of downsides when it is boundaryless 24/7. Boundaryless flexibility increasingly "passes the buck" by shifting the burden of matching customers' schedule demands onto workers, depleting personal time, and—for teleworkers—transferring workspace and tech support costs as well. Employees are at greater risk for layoffs, lower ratings, and lower pay because they are less socially connected to colleagues. The work-without-boundaries approach may also increase isolation, symptoms of depression, overwork, and job creep into nonwork space and time.

What happens at home matters to the success of boundaryless working. Early studies that reported better work-life balance under its conditions typically held domestic and work hours constant, which may have hidden the gender effects. As recent reviews suggest, an employee (often a woman) who is teleworking is more likely to take on even more family demands and report greater work-life conflict.

This increase in work-nonwork multitasking while teleworking has become visible during the Covid-19 crisis, culminating in a global "shecession." Even for dual-career couples, traditional gender roles persisted at home, aggravated by pandemic disruptions. A national study of woman scientists found that although their mostly male partners also worked remotely during the pandemic, the women ended up doing 90% of the domestic labor. Fathers were unable or unwilling to help, so working women managed virtual schooling, childcare, pets, cooking, and cleaning, and experienced higher work-family conflict and overload. This exacerbated the gender gap, which, the World Economic Forum notes, has increased by more than an entire generation's worth: It will now take 135.6 years for women to reach parity with men, rather than 99.5. Gendered inequality will continue in the post-pandemic workplace unless organizations change their approach.

So, is hybrid the magic flexibility pill?

As companies move to implement a post-pandemic hybrid flexibility—a largely employer-determined mix of remote and office work schedules, incorporating a blend of unique accommodations and widespread boundaryless work with little or no structure—employees' well-being and careers could actually suffer harm. We believe that women and those with health or family-care needs would be the most disadvantaged. That's because the majority of these arrangements won't effectively empower employees to align job and nonwork demands by controlling when and where they work. Our fear is that companies may end up offering *inflexible* flexibility, whereby employees have little choice about schedules and which days they may work remotely. At the other extreme, flexibility will be implemented without structures or norms, resulting in a "program" that is disorganized, scattershot, and reactive to work requirements. Expectations about where and when one should work may shift without warning, as work seeps into off-hours and employees struggle to live predictable nonwork lives.

True flexibility will require truly new thinking.

A Better Way

True flexibility aligns employers and employees to achieve mutual gain in meeting both performance and work-life needs: It is a means to compete in the market over the long term, and it gives employees a say and some choice in how flexibility is implemented on their teams and in their organizations.

This is both a top-down and a bottom-up process. Leaders listen, set goals, and provide resources to make flexibility possible. Employees choose flexible working that suits their needs while communicating with their managers and colleagues to ensure that team, client, and customer requirements are met. In other words, the company provides the scaffolding—flexibility options, equipment, and supportive performance-management systems—and individual employees and teams decide how to organize their work within it.

With this approach, employers benefit by retaining a globally diverse, sustainable workforce. Employees experience well-being, enjoy respectful team processes, and avoid burnout and health problems. But it requires moving away from old narratives and enhancing employee support and trust. To do that, leaders must first assess their current culture. How do they define flexibility? Has the company leaned more toward accommodation, boundarylessness, or a combination? What policies has it embraced, and for which jobs? Then they can assess which true flexibility principles should be further embraced. We detail those principles here.

Make flexibility available to all employees

Every job deserves some flexibility. Even if telework isn't always an option, organizations should offer flexibility to both office and frontline workers. It cannot be viewed as a scarce or privileged resource. Yet all too often that's what happens. Companies ignore the needs of essential and hourly workers, providing flexibility only to knowledge workers on technology-driven teams.

Consider a pharmaceutical company that was part of one of our studies. During a snowstorm, senior directors and managers could work from home, but secretaries were forced to drive on a busy (and icy) freeway to get to the office. Many leaders didn't realize that they had such an unfair policy, because they were accustomed to administrative support in a hierarchical culture. The company gradually expanded its flexibility by experimenting with summer hours: A secretary could partner with a peer to cover each other's Friday workload, enabling them to take every other Friday off.

Flexibility for all workers is indeed possible. As managers learned during the pandemic, a company can schedule hourly work flexibly and in shorter shifts and give paid time off at the last minute without penalty; in fact, those accommodations were necessary to support essential workers during the crisis. We know of an engine manufacturer that, even before Covid-19, regularly scheduled highly cross-trained "floaters" who could rotate jobs and shifts on teams and fill in wherever colleagues need help. That allowed its teams to function well during the pandemic, when workers had to care for children during school closures or take care of other personal needs. McDonald's recently added paid time off and an emergency childcare program to attract mostly hourly workers. Another example comes from a busy metropolitan police department: Officers, including supervisors, were able to use predetermined compressed workweeks to create more-predictable schedules and allow for recovery time.

Increasing flexibility for frontline workers can help a company better support diversity and inclusion, because immigrants, people of color, and working mothers are heavily represented in service industries. Ultimately, all employees need to be supported in their personal lives. If your flexibility policies exclude a segment of your workforce, you're doing something wrong.

Prioritize clear structures and policies

If you were to randomly ask leaders or employees at your company to describe flexibility, they should be able to give a clear answer— and their answers should be consistent. Flexibility policies will not work if they are difficult to understand, if employees or managers don't know how to use them, or if they vary greatly in approach. Organizations benefit when they develop clear written frameworks with principles that can guide decision-making about and expectations for flexibility. These frameworks should be communicated widely.

As an example, here's a brief checklist that draws from the employee assistance program at LifeWorks (formerly Morneau

Shepell) and can serve as a starting point for any company's flexible work arrangements:

- Develop a written policy that clearly lays out expectations.

- Communicate with all employees about the possibilities for flexible work and aim to achieve equality.

- Ask employees to document their planned versus actual work hours to foster work routines and increase transparency about when they are working and when they are off.

- Use clear metrics to evaluate employees on the *quality* of their work, not the timing or quantity of it.

Manager checklists like this one are becoming widespread. Consider this example from Canada, where, as in the United Kingdom and Australia, the right to request a flexible schedule is gaining legal ground.

Within these guidelines, the manager's role is to match flexible work processes with customer, product creation, and service demands. Thus leaders must understand how each type of flexibility—schedule, place, continuity, workload, and mode—aligns with the job at hand, their employees, and policies. As the exhibit "A flexibility primer" shows, various combinations of flexible arrangements may have bundling synergies. For example, location and schedule flexibility sometimes work well in combination.

The choices made must be viewed as fair by both leaders and employees. Studies show that when they are, workers who experience work-family conflict nonetheless remain committed to their organizations.

How can managers cultivate this kind of environment and roll out flexible policies fairly? One way is to develop a team charter, as the financial services firm Northern Trust did for units migrating to a flexible work mode. Questions that leaders, team members, and other stakeholders might discuss include:

- How has the company decided to manage location-based pay equity? For example, will all fully remote workers who perform the same jobs, regardless of whether they live in Tulsa or Los Angeles, receive the same base and merit pay?

FIGURE 1-1

A flexibility primer

A look at five different types of flexibility your organization can consider and how they might be bundled.

Policy type	Policy examples	Bundling option	Employee benefits	Employer benefits
Schedule Employees can vary their schedules to meet daily, weekly, or monthly expectations.	·Flex time ·Compressed workweek ·Shift swapping ·Shift scheduling	Schedule Place Continuity Workload	·More control over days or hours worked ·Less time commuting ·Greater ability to meet nonwork needs during regular work hours ·Greater feeling of control	·Greater productivity and employee focus ·Less absenteeism ·Less overtime
Place Employees can work away from their employer's work site using technology or other types of communication.	·Telework (using technology to work from any location) ·Remote work (living outside the geographic area of the employer) ·Telecommuting (working from home) ·Hoteling/ satellite offices	Schedule Place	·Less time commuting locally ·Less exhaustion from global or national trips ·Freedom to live closer to family or friends	·Less turnover ·Lower overhead costs ·Larger talent pool
Continuity Employees can choose when to take time off without losing their jobs.	·Leaves (family, sick, maternity, paternity, education, military)	Schedule Continuity Workload	·Time to give birth, care for a child or parent, attend school, serve in the military, or recover from illness ·Ability to return to work sooner when combined with job sharing or part-time work ·Less burnout ·Time to nurse or bond with a child	·Less turnover ·Retention of quality employees

Policy type	Policy examples	Bundling option	Employee benefits	Employer benefits
Workload Employees can opt for a less-than-full-time schedule in return for a commensurate cut in pay.	·Job share ·Part-time work ·Lighter workload	Schedule Workload	·Less overload or burnout ·Decreased work-family conflict	·Less turnover ·Greater retention of quality employees
Mode Employees can vary the degree to which they work off-site.	·Site work ·Hybrid ·Remote	Schedule Place Continuity Workload Mode	·Ability to coordinate and accomplish work using technology ·Ability to mix modes for varying types of work tasks	·Greater productivity ·Lower office space costs

Source: "Flexible Work Schedules," by E. E. Kossek and J. S. Michel (2009); "A Review of Telework Research," by D. E. Bailey and N. B. Kurland; and "Balanced Flexibility," by E. E. Kossek, R. Thompson, and B. Lautsch (2015).

- What are fair criteria for how the team sets core hours—say, from 10 to 3—when members will be available for collaboration, meetings, and communication?

- What is an equitable way to set limits on employees' availability, and what are norms for respecting time off?

Although clear policies and consistent implementation are important, overly restrictive policies are not the answer. Processes should be adaptable.

Empower employees to create and manage their own flexibility

Although leaders must help shape the structures and policies for flexible work, they don't need to have all the answers. Instead they should facilitate conversations with workers to unpack all the ways in which people interpret flexibility—from where one works to the construction of one's work schedule. It may be helpful for managers to give employees a list of considerations to reflect on and address.

- How might my clients' experience be affected by my flexibility? In what ways can any negative impact be mitigated?

- How might my interactions with team members be affected? What actions can I take to ensure strong collaboration and working relationships?

- Do I have, or can I develop, the skills I need for the proposed flexible work arrangement? For example, do I have the self-discipline to manage attention and boundaries for telework or to maintain the energy and focus for a compressed workweek? Have I talked with my manager and clients to ensure that my part-time job is designed and scoped realistically so that I can perform it effectively within my reduced hours?

- Do I have the right work and home resources (tech support, an internet connection, space, family support, a backup work location) to ensure that I can accomplish my job?

Sometimes managers also provide checklists to employees who are using specific types of flexibility. Some examples are the Australian government's tips for working out of the office, Salesforce's guidelines prior to a leave of absence, and Tettra's onboarding tips for remote workers.

The next step is to create organization-wide structures for self-scheduling and shift-swapping to empower employees. Rather than making supervisors pivotal in managing the everyday implementation of flexibility, some industries are setting up employee self-management processes that give workers greater control over their schedules and hours without penalty.

Health care organizations in particular, with their large female workforce, have been early adopters of self-scheduling. In one study of self-scheduling among nurses in five comparable medical and surgical units, a key component was educating them about self-scheduling and negotiation skills and when to adjust guidelines to meet needs such as determining holiday coverage. Employee satisfaction and retention increased as a result.

Another example comes from Delta, a large nonunionized U.S. airline that employs a "bidding" process whereby employees pick their own shifts using a software program, with choice increasing according to seniority. Workers may swap or give away shifts as long as overtime doesn't increase and health and safety rules are not violated.

In both these examples the role of leaders is to establish guidelines regarding what works and what doesn't in a way that is facilitating but not controlling, ensuring that workers understand their accountability for guaranteeing staffing mandates and, in the case of health care, the quality of patient care. Companies moving to widespread flexible remote-work systems can learn a lot from them.

Remove disincentives for use

Policies that enable employees to take vacation when desired or sick leave when needed—even when that time off is unlimited on paper—are often accompanied by disincentives for using them. (Consider the "unlimited vacation time" that no one actually takes advantage of.) A common barrier is chronic understaffing. In a study we conducted of frontline workers, only one in four employees at a continuously running oil-production company could use available vacation time because of it. As a result, employees suffered burnout. One manager reported being unable to get time off to attend a niece's wedding, even though he was supposed to walk her down the aisle in place of her late father. We also see structural disincentives in health care, where nurses are increasingly unable to use paid vacation and sick time earned, and we have encountered leave incentive programs in which employees can actually make *more* money by not taking time off.

Many organizational cultures disincentivize the use of time-off policies for nonwork needs as well. In one case, a department chair celebrated a male professor for attending a faculty meeting during parental leave, whereas a female colleague, who had just given birth, missed the meeting to nurse the baby and recover. The message to employees was clear: You are rewarded for showing up even when the official policy says you're not supposed to.

Leaders must remove both types of disincentives. One tactic is to publicly recognize top talent who work flexibly and achieve high performance. In one of our studies, a lawyer who was working reduced hours won an Employee of the Year award by discovering a way to save the firm a great deal of money.

We've also seen some companies use flexibility as an incentive to reduce excessive overtime and burnout and increase productivity and cost savings. One pharmaceutical company offered employees workweeks of four 10-hour days with job security in return for a no-overtime-payment agreement. The company saved money *and* saw improved performance as the team became self-managing and supervisors transitioned out of boss roles and became team members themselves. The former supervisors responded positively because they no longer had to manage the overtime needs of the organization, could work just four days a week, and felt more integrated and supported on their teams.

Remember that leadership matters

True flexibility that meets business and personal needs is unlikely to succeed without support from the top. An example comes from GM CEO Mary Barra's post-pandemic call to "work appropriately." "Where the work permits," she said, "employees have the flexibility to work where they can have the greatest impact on achieving our goals. . . . It is up to leaders to focus on the work, not the where, and we will provide the tools and resources needed to make the right decisions to support our teams."

The jury is still out on how successful GM and other firms—such as Google—that take similar approaches will be, but it's encouraging to hear CEOs strategically setting the tone for flexibility by making it the rule rather than the exception. Top leaders can also recognize and reward supervisors who encourage their teams to get the work done without burning out.

Leaders must be careful how they talk about various forms of flexibility. For example, when teleworking is framed as an initiative to improve work-family balance, it often becomes a gendered phenomenon, leading men to assume they can't take advantage of it or to conceal that they're doing it for work-life reasons to avoid being stigmatized. So it's important to communicate examples of increased flexibility's effectiveness for all kinds of workers in all kinds of jobs and at all levels.

Leaders must also explain the organization's commitment to flexibility to outside stakeholders. For example, if a company is practicing flexibility but its clients still expect 24/7 responses, the company's policy simply won't work. One way to address this issue is to bake client expectations into flexible work plans—for example, by staffing key accounts with several employees who can tag-team and then presenting that as a benefit to clients.

Experiment and measure outcomes, including equity

True flexibility is an ongoing process requiring that management be open to experimentation and new ideas. Some arrangements may not work at first and will need to be adjusted. That is normal and an important part of the process; evolution does not equate to failure. For example, Microsoft found that when a large team initially moved to remote work in 2020, employees worked an average of four more hours a week, sent more messages at non-standard hours, and spent more time in meetings (albeit shorter ones), risking burnout. Leaders soon realized that this pace was unsustainable—for themselves and for employees—and encouraged teams to develop guidelines to ensure both work and non-work time (clear-cut shifts, daily breaks, and dedicated solo work hours, for example).

At the same time, evidence suggests that gathering data and making changes can pay off. Northern Trust migrated entire job functions and teams to hybrid remote work (with at least one day in the office and at least one day at home) years before the pandemic. It used pre- and post-evaluation tools to assess whether jobs could be done securely and teams could work effectively regardless of location. Migrating, piloting, and evaluating departments one at a time, the company shifted its culture toward more-flexible working by systematically accumulating data confirming its approach while fine-tuning for each work unit. It saved millions of dollars by reducing office space around the world, and employee stress plummeted as a result of fewer commutes.

Consider the impact of flexibility on your global workforce

In interviews at an oil company headquartered in the EU, we found that employees in one of its Asian offices preferred a 3 p.m. to 12 a.m. workday. That allowed many workers to pick up their children from school beforehand. It also facilitated communication across time zones and increased employee productivity and engagement. For example, no one had to get up in the middle of the night for a conference call, since 3 p.m. in the Asia office was 9 a.m. at the company's headquarters. Such localized flexibility practices can help maintain equity among employees in different parts of the world so that team members work at mutually convenient times.

To ensure fair access and results as your company experiments, start by taking race and gender into consideration while conducting an audit to see whether heavier users of work-life flexibility have pay equity. There's evidence that inequity can and does occur. For instance, in 2019 the bonuses of senior female employees at the Swiss bank UBS were not restored to previous levels when the women returned from maternity leave. Some of them eventually resigned. Another example comes from Nike, which cut pay for star athletes who went on maternity leave. (After a backlash, the company adjusted that policy to avoid penalizing mothers.)

We also caution against establishing a policy that offers employees the option of remote work only if they take a pay cut, or creating a pay structure that's based on location. Talent is talent, and compensation shouldn't depend on where employees are unless their location is vital for the people they're serving (say, in government) or required by licensing rules (say, in law). Such policies are also likely to make the shecession even worse and increase the gender pay gap, because women are 50% more likely than men to apply for remote work. They also use flexibility more often, take on more school and childcare logistical management during the workday, and are more likely to be the trailing spouse when couples coordinate dual careers, thus trading geographical location for remote work.

Finally, remember that implementing flexibility involves a learning curve

The leader's role is to make performance expectations clear and resources to support flexibility and performance consistent across people and teams. If someone is falling short, put that person on a performance-improvement plan and assess whether skills, motivation, or some other issue is getting in the way. Don't assume that flexibility is the main reason that work isn't getting done.

The pandemic has led many employees to rethink the importance of work in their lives and to change their relationship to it. Many are demanding more flexibility. In response, leaders need to stop viewing flexibility as an HR policy and regard it as an opportunity for organizational transformation that will benefit both their employees and their businesses.

---

12 Questions About Hybrid Work, Answered

Advice on inclusivity, onboarding, performance measurement, and more. **by Tsedal Neeley**

Extensive data across surveys indicate that most people want hybrid work arrangements—that is, a mix of in-person and remote work—as we continue to move through the pandemic. For example, Microsoft's 2021 Work Trend Index, a study of over 30,000 people in 31 countries, found that 73% of respondents desire remote work options. FlexJobs surveyed more than 2,100 people who worked remotely during the pandemic and found that 58% would leave their jobs if they weren't able to continue working from home at least some of the time.

The reasons aren't surprising. Remote work has allowed people to eliminate stressful commutes, reduce daily expenses, and increase quality time with family and friends. At the same time, many workers miss their colleagues, the camaraderie of the office, and the learning opportunities that come from serendipitous interactions. Questions about whether physical presence in the office is necessary for career advancement loom large as well. And ultimately, shifting to hybrid work marks a radical change for most organizations.

At the beginning of the pandemic, I answered HBR subscribers' most pressing questions about the sudden shift to remote work. Recently I called on readers again to send me their questions about transitioning to hybrid work. I've answered the most frequently asked ones here. They cover everything from inclusive hybrid planning to onboarding; measuring performance to fostering connection and trust; and using digital tools effectively while also fortifying cybersecurity and transforming physical spaces. It's an essential guide for any leader managing this transition.

1. What's the best way to approach hybrid work designs?

Leaders need to design plans that combine the preferences of their workforce and the core work that their organization needs to do well—and they need to be prepared to adjust as they go. Here's how.

Survey everyone anonymously about preferences and intentions to leave

Ask questions that will help you gather insights about tasks employees believe require in-person versus virtual presence, and gauge the number of remote days people might want each week. In addition, assess whether employees would want to relocate if they could work from anywhere; this will help you anticipate whether you need to consider developing a policy for it.

You should also pose questions about people's intentions to leave if work arrangements aren't in line with their needs: "To what extent are you thinking of leaving this organization? To what extent do you plan to ask people about new opportunities? To what extent are you planning to look for a new job if you're unsatisfied with your work arrangement?"

Identify the principles for hybrid guidelines

Based on your data analyses and the core work of the organization, determine and convey the operating principles for your hybrid policy. Examples of guiding principles may include expectations that in-person days are needed for onboarding new hires, specific collaboration efforts, periodically enhancing connections with coworkers, and performing select innovation activities. Of course, some companies may find that those very activities can be carried out virtually depending on their culture, products, and services. The point is that each organization should identify the approach that best serves its stakeholders. As you develop yours, keep in mind that people resent having to go into the office to stare at a screen or be on video calls that they could have taken from home.

There isn't a one-size-fits-all path, but having principles centralized from the top will ensure equity and consistent planning across groups. Teams will then have to interpret the policy for themselves—though their interpretations must be equitable and in line with the organization's principles and needs. For example, PepsiCo's Work That Works program is designed to give teams that kind of autonomy.

Convey that the new work approach will be adjusted over time

Hybrid implementations will be subject to change as people learn what is effective for all stakeholders in a fast-changing societal landscape. Accordingly, set expectations that adjustments will be made through trials and learnings. Doing so will allay anxiety about the permanence of suboptimal arrangements. Some companies' recent adjustments include suggesting overall percentages of in-person or remote days per week rather than prescribing a specific number (Uber) and offering permanent remote options in addition to hybrid plans (LinkedIn).

Likewise, ideal in-person activity choices for a given group will crystallize with experimentation. For example, it might work best for a team to meet for several consecutive days in person for the launch of a product and then work remotely for the subsequent weeks. People will inevitably test and improve on their approaches.

2. How can we be as inclusive as possible in hybrid work designs?

Hybrid work can create inclusion issues for organizations. Leaders have to think creatively to enable on-site-essential employees to work remotely some days. Even medical doctors have been able to do this. Here are two options that can include the most people.

Pooling and rotating

If workers have similar tasks that must be done in person, one approach is to pool and rotate the work to reduce the number of people who have to be on-site simultaneously. This requires appraising the responsibilities of a group as an interdependent system. For example, if there are seven IT professionals responsible for the operations of control rooms, enabling each person to work from home one or two days per week while the others provide coverage can maximize opportunities for everyone.

Once this paradigm shift is in play, it often becomes apparent that everyone has some tasks that don't require in-person presence. In some cases, organizations have enhanced their technical capabilities to allow the remote execution of tasks that had traditionally been tied to buildings. For example, many digitized analog materials that were previously available only on-site and implemented VPNs to enable their access virtually.

Providing remote learning days

For team members whose jobs are inextricably tied to physical spaces, allotting remote learning days—that can be used for either online or in-person classes, as well as other skill-building apprenticeships—has proven to be a powerful act of inclusion. The number of remote learning days each year will vary by group or organization, but the idea is to ensure that everyone has days for remote self-development. The added bonus is that organizations are investing in all employees, which increases people's capabilities and loyalty.

3. How can we help people transition to a hybrid work environment?

All teams transitioning to hybrid work have to start with a formal launch by explicitly planning the team's journey. Managers should hold launch discussions that can last up to two hours to get everyone aligned in four areas:

- Shared goals that make clear the aims the team is pursuing
- Shared understanding about individual roles, constraints, and potential to contribute
- Shared understanding of available resources, ranging from information to budgets
- Shared norms that map out how the group will collaborate effectively with digital tools, as well as how the group will remain connected personally and professionally

And since hybrid collaborators are dispersed, you also need periodic relaunches to drive performance. A relaunch appraises how the group is faring while also addressing what can make it better. I recommend a cadence of every six to eight weeks to stay abreast of evolving dynamics, such as integrating a new digital tool, responding to a sudden shift in the market, or onboarding a new team member.

4. What are best practices for remote onboarding?

Starting a new job away from a collocated office can be isolating for new hires, whether their teams are hybrid or full-time remote. That's why having a robust, monthlong plan to onboard and integrate employees is essential. Of course, bringing in a cohort together can offer an enduring shared journey for newcomers. However, a single newcomer can still feel well integrated with deliberate planning.

Welcoming and acculturating new employees is a team effort. During this monthlong period, the new hire should never be left alone—each day they should have activities with others in the company. Managers need to provide a diverse list of key members of the organization for the newcomer to meet beyond their immediate team, as a way to establish their internal network. Assigning a virtual onboarding buddy, often a peer, who checks in regularly and can answer any questions a new hire may feel uncomfortable asking the boss has proven to be very effective. Group learning opportunities also promote bonding with existing members of the team.

Ensure the new hire has sufficient tech, too. Although it may sound obvious, a company that has not invested in the technology necessary for onboarding new hires and committed IT support throughout the process may make a poor first impression. Technology is a primary engagement channel to a company, and poor deployment for new hires can be fundamentally alienating.

5. How do we ensure that proximity bias doesn't affect career advancement?

In order for hybrid work to actually work, managers have to understand that out of sight doesn't mean out of mind. Remote members of a hybrid team will often wonder whether they fare differently than collocated workers who can catch the boss's ear in person. For example, they may worry they will be evaluated more harshly or given lower performance reviews than their in-office peers. It's incumbent upon managers to ensure that these fears are not realized.

Providing adequate feedback, and developing and promoting people without proximity bias, is crucial. Working remotely won't have a negative impact on relationships or the task dimensions of job performance so long as managers' evaluations of remote workers are as fair as those of collocated ones.

6. How do we measure the performance of remote or hybrid employees?

The great remote work experiment disrupted companies' reliance on butts-in-seats presenteeism to measure performance. When managers aren't in the same space as their teams most of the time, they instead have to measure performance based on outcomes, group cohesion, and individual development.

First, assess whether people are *delivering results*—in other words, achieving expected goals. Second, ensure the team is *operating as one cohesive unit*. Learning how to work together as a group, rather than as individuals in silos, is what creates a successful hybrid team. Finally, support *individual growth* as a function of being on the team. When team members have the space to grow, expand their knowledge, acquire new skills, and learn new perspectives, their job satisfaction increases and they become more capable.

Once goals in all three areas are clearly in place, managers have to empower, equip, coach, and assess performance according to outcomes instead of micromanaging every single task.

7. How can we foster trust among teammates who seldom see one another in person?

Just like groups, trust comes in many shapes and sizes. In-person teams start from our more natural mindset of being cautiously skeptical and building trust over time, but hybrid or remote groups have to flip the script: Start from a mindset of having confident trust in one another, and work from there. Sure, challenges could arise that shake our trust, in which case we need to adjust our expectations. But it's much more likely that people will prove us right, because trust inspires trust. It's a virtuous cycle.

Two types of trust have proven to be most effective in groups of people who don't share the same space routinely: *cognitive swift trust* and *emotional trust*. Cognitive swift trust is the willingness of team members to depend on one another based on sufficient evidence of reliability and competence. While swift trust isn't as complete as what's built when people are able to get to know one another over time, it's sufficient for completing shared tasks effectively.

By comparison, emotional trust is grounded in the belief that coworkers and managers have care and concern for us. When that kind of trust is present, people feel connection, a sense of closeness. As Theodore Roosevelt famously said, "People don't care how much you know until they know how much you care." Empathetic words, actions, and self-disclosures that occur in meetings, emails, chats, or online posts can nurture emotional trust.

Managers of hybrid groups can also feed trust with activities during structured unstructured time that make members more familiar with one another's personalities and values. These exchanges may occur more informally when everyone is colocated, but they can still be facilitated through virtual lunches, happy hours, coffee chats, or online games.

8. How can we eliminate tech exhaustion?

Leaders designing hybrid and remote work options have to understand that different tools support different goals and come with distinct benefits and limitations. Complaints of depletion, headaches, and even the slurring of words can occur if employees are going from one video call to the next. Just because videoconferencing is a good option for remote meetings doesn't mean you should use it for most occasions, and just because video tools allow you to fully pack your calendar doesn't mean you should.

It's crucial for managers to mix up the digital tools they use, as well as to create periods of transition between meetings and to consider reducing their length. Remember Parkinson's law: We fill the amount of time we allocate to meetings. If we plan to cover a topic in an hour, we will fill that hour to meet our goals. If we cut that number in half, we will achieve our goals in that reduced time frame.

9. How do we match digital tools with work needs?

Tech experts place digital tools on a spectrum from lean to rich media and from synchronous to asynchronous.

Lean media, such as email, convey less information and context, whereas rich media, such as video and face-to-face interaction, convey more information and context. Lean media tend to be asynchronous and are more effective in situations that require the straightforward transmission of information. Rich media are usually synchronous and are appropriate for situations with more ambiguity.

Lean media tend to work well for teams with close relationships, because they already know one another and don't need added context, and for teams with tension, because they can minimize exposure to potential conflict. Newer teams without any history, on the other hand, benefit more from rich media's added context.

Lean media are also great for routine tasks, such as record keeping, while rich media are usually better for nonroutine tasks, such as brainstorming and creative development (writing, designing, and so on).

Deciding which mode is best for which items in the workday—whether it's a quick question, a project proposal, or a brainstorming session—is an ongoing process. Managers must include the whole team in discussions about which to use going forward.

10. How should leaders rethink office spaces for in-person work?

Hybrid work is transforming the physical design of office spaces to promote connection, collaboration, and innovation. The key question of workplace design is: What kind of space will bring people out of the comfort of their home desks and into the office?

The answer, according to Meena Krenek, principal and interior design director of architecture firm Perkins and Will in Los Angeles, is a holistic approach that seeks to create experiences that allow people to thrive at the intersection of *people* and *technology*. As a first step, Krenek says, understand people's evolving perspectives, needs, and preferences in the workplace through survey data collected by the company.

Broadly, however, Krenek emphasizes that the hybrid world requires our offices to become a destination, not a default. To make the commute worth it, these workspaces emphasize form over function: less office cubicle and more café lounge, with amenities like cozy furniture, gourmet coffee, natural light, good ventilation, and outdoor patios. Optimal conditions for video calls, such as state-of-the-art monitors, headsets and speakers, and studio lighting, will also be key differentiators.

These hybrid spaces will look different from the familiar grid of personal desks and meeting spaces for small groups. Their key feature is *fluidity*: Rooms become hackable spaces that people can reconfigure to accommodate a specific meeting or task, from 12-person brainstorming sessions to private client meetings. A bookcase on casters or a semitransparent curtain can become a movable wall. Smart boards that function as writable surfaces float in and out of spaces as needed. Whiteboards, on the other hand, may be a thing of the past because they don't enable the digital capturing, storing, and reusing of collective work. Pilot programs for these kinds of office spaces can help leaders learn employees' patterns and preferences when using them.

11. How do we keep our data and systems safe when people are working from anywhere?

A recent HP study of over 8,000 office workers revealed that around 70% are using their work devices for personal tasks and vice versa. As a result, employees working from home are increasingly targeted by hackers; global cyberattacks increased a whopping 238% during the pandemic. Phishing and scan-and-exploit attacks are greater threats when people aren't within the physical walls of a firm. The old "moat and castle" approach, in which companies secure the perimeter of their office's local network, is no longer sufficient for remote and hybrid teams. In fact, it's been counterproductive for years. Long and innumerable passwords and VPNs that bring internet speeds to a crawl are impediments to people's productivity when they're remote. In turn, they use unauthorized devices and find workarounds that make them prime targets for cyberattacks.

In a remote-hybrid world, the access point for bad actors can be employees themselves (think phishing emails), not just the network architecture (think viruses getting past a firewall). All nonwork devices used at home are potential attack vectors, especially for executives. This demands an approach that addresses the full range of access points individually, from corporate laptops to personal smartphones. Centralized policies have to be clear to everyone and flexible enough to secure many different devices while maintaining a baseline for protection. For some, corporate-owned devices may be the only means to access critical data; these people should get priority on security patches.

Cybersecurity policies must also provide visibility into user behavior while at the same time balancing the impact on employee experience and privacy. Security experts urge a regular review of who has access to data and for how long. This is what's called *least privileged access*, which sets clear boundaries for each employee's minimum access to data.

Finally, hybrid leaders have to prioritize training employees in cybersecurity so that everyone knows how to spot and avoid attacks.

12. What might the future of hybrid work look like?

Hybrid work is not just about changing the location of the workplace. It's also about changing our most fundamental routines to become more efficient and optimized.

This will include evolving from leading and collaborating primarily with people to doing so with machines as well. It means thinking further into the future about how to use emerging technologies such as artificial intelligence, machine learning, and robotic process automation (RPA). It also suggests that the nature of work will evolve to include the automation of everyday repetitive tasks that steal time away from the more open-ended, higher-concept work of innovation.

In that sense, hybrid work will increasingly be defined by how we work with machines. Everything is up for grabs. I anticipate that the processes that are most ingrained in a company's workflows today will be taken apart and rebuilt from the ground up with new tools and goals.

Sidney Madison Prescott, global head of intelligent automation at Spotify and coauthor of a how-to guide for RPA business solutions, refers to the automation of repetitive tasks as *human augmentation* because it ultimately gives us more time to do the things that only humans can do: thinking, ideating, creating. As she puts it, human augmentation begins with reexamining the most routine processes we've long accepted as just part of the job. And this goes for every single role, from engineers to business analysts to salespeople. For example, the accepted workflow for an accountant might include many hours spent consolidating countless reports and triple-checking for human errors that inevitably creep in. An RPA tool can automate the whole process, freeing the accountant up for other work, significantly reducing the rate of human error, and making the task more shareable with teammates. Once the tool has proven effective, it could then be adapted to automate similar processes.

Migrating to hybrid work is often cast as a question of in-person versus remote options, with time and space being the core elements of concern. The mindset shift that hybrid work requires, and the changes we make because of it, will serve us well as the digital revolution further changes the nature of work through data and technology.

A Guide to Implementing the Four-Day Workweek

Working less can reduce employees' stress—without sacrificing productivity. *by Ashley Whillans and Charlotte Lockhart*

In June of this year, Kickstarter became the latest in a string of organizations to announce they are experimenting with a four-day workweek. Its employees will be working 32 rather than 40 hours per week, while being expected to achieve the same productivity levels and earning the same pay. Though some recent studies on the efficacy of the four-day week have been overblown in the media, research suggests that reducing work hours can decrease employee stress and improve well-being without impacting productivity—but only when implemented effectively.

So, what does that look like? One of us (Ashley) is an academic researcher focused on time, money, and happiness, and the other (Charlotte) is the CEO of a global nonprofit that funds research on four-day workweek practices and the future of work. We've created a six-step guide to help organizations plan and roll out a reduction in working hours. While our focus in this piece is on office-centric knowledge jobs, we believe our recommendations can apply to any company where adjusting work hours is possible.

Step 1: Shift Your Mindset

Psychological research suggests that most of us are "medium maximizers"—we tend to focus on objective, easily quantifiable success metrics such as hours worked, rather than more qualitative metrics such as productivity or well-being. As a result, many companies use immediate responsiveness and time at the office as proxies for employees' commitment levels, even when those measures seldom correspond to actual value added to the organization.

For a four-day workweek to be successful, leaders must shift their mindsets to value actual productivity, not just hours worked. They must ensure that employees aren't worried they will be penalized for prioritizing work-life balance, and that starts with modeling a healthier work-life balance themselves. Ashley's research has found that explicitly framing a reduced-work initiative as a companywide policy rather than an informal or optional project can go a long way in encouraging this critical mindset shift.

In addition, leaders must embrace the uncertainty that comes with trying out a new initiative. The first mistake we've seen many managers make is attempting to anticipate all possible problems and eliminate all possible sources of risk before the pilot even begins. While planning is important, falling into decision inertia helps no one—and real problem solving is only possible through trial and error, not in closed-door conversations among leadership.

This also means accepting that some people won't like the changes and some might even quit as a result. That's OK. Managers should openly acknowledge that the new plan might not work for everyone. Remember: When one employee leaves, it creates room for others who buy into the new culture, ultimately strengthening the team and the business.

Step 2: Define Your Goals and Metrics

Once you've decided that your organization is ready to make a change, it's time to start planning. Both employees and leaders should be actively involved in a number of critical decisions. One company Charlotte and her team worked with formed an employee-driven subcommittee to spearhead the rollout of its reduced-hours program. The small working group (lovingly nicknamed the "pessi-mist committee") met for an hour each day for six weeks to discuss potential problems before launching the pilot.

Based on this and other case studies, here are some questions that we've found can be helpful to consider:

Questions for employees:

- Should we work four eight-hour days, or reduced hours on five days?
- Which days or hours should we take off?
- How can we keep the change from negatively impacting our clients, customers, and other stakeholders?
- What steps can we take to increase our productivity?
- How will we share our ideas for process improvements with one another?

Questions for leadership:

- How will the organization measure productivity?

- What support will employees need to make this pilot a success?

- How long should the organization run this pilot?

- Are there any legal concerns we should be aware of?

As a part of these conversations, it will be critical to consider how you will measure the success of the program in relation to the goals you identify. That includes outcomes you hope will change, such as employee happiness, as well as outcomes you hope *won't* change, such as client satisfaction and productivity.

Step 3: Communicate Internally and Externally

Next, think through your communication plan. There are a number of concerns that are likely on the minds of internal and external stakeholders, and it's important for leaders to be proactive in addressing them.

Internally, the biggest questions will probably be around how the change will affect people's jobs. Be clear about your reasons for trying out the four-day workweek, and assure your employees that they will not be laid off, experience a pay cut, or lose out on other benefits like paid vacation.

In addition, it's likely that reducing work hours will necessitate changes to some internal processes and norms, so it's important to discuss that up front. For example, at one organization we worked with, employees introduced weekly 30-minute meetings to cover everything that had previously been discussed in less efficient, ad hoc meetings, which reduced interruptions and thus increased "heads-down" work time. In fact, Ashley's recent research found that the pandemic made some knowledge workers more efficient, in part because it forced them to be more deliberate in scheduling collaboration time.

Every organization is different, so encourage conversations about how to get more done in less time—whether that's by implementing new tools, eliminating unnecessary meetings, or making existing meetings more effective.

The same is true externally. Many companies worry what their clients will think if they reduce hours, but those worries can often be assuaged with a simple conversation. Identify which customers, partners, or other stakeholders might be affected, and work with the appropriate internal representatives to ensure the scheduling change is communicated clearly.

In many cases, you'll be surprised by how receptive the external party is. During one of Ashley's studies, employees engaged in a time-blocking experiment that made them unavailable to everyone, including their clients, for hours or even full days at a time. Despite managers' fears, both the employees and their clients reported higher levels of satisfaction than before the shift.

Step 4: Run a Pilot

You've decided, you've planned, you've communicated—it's time to act! Remember that in the pilot stage, the goal isn't to get everything right from the start, but rather to identify the tools and processes your organization needs to make reduced work hours possible. You will likely need at least a few months to implement a full-scale pilot study. During this time, problems will arise. Try your best to address them as they happen, knowing that full-scale solutions might have to wait until the pilot is over. View any issues not as indicators of failure, but as opportunities to improve and fine-tune your implementation plan. Some questions we've seen come out of pilot programs include:

- What are the boundaries I need to put in place for myself and my team?

- What assistance do I need from leadership to accomplish a reduced work schedule?

- What will happen to team activities like "cake Fridays"?

Creating an environment in which people feel safe asking these questions—yes, even about your workplace dessert rituals—is an essential ingredient for a successful pilot. Trust that your employees are doing their best to make good decisions, and support them as they try out different methods to increase their effectiveness.

Step 5: Assess the Pilot

Once the pilot is complete, there are a number of ways you can analyze the results. First, there are both qualitative and quantitative metrics that can help you understand how the pilot impacted employee well-being.

Qualitatively, group interviews can provide insight into employees' experiences with the four-day workweek, and more-formalized job satisfaction surveys can identify trends and changes in self-reported levels of stress, work-life balance, and quality of life. Quantitatively, there are other metrics you can look at. For example, did employees take fewer sick days during the pilot? If so, this might suggest that employees felt less burned out.

As far as productivity, the relevant metrics will depend on the team. On sales teams, it might make sense to focus on the number of deals created, conversion rates, or average closing times. On creative teams, you can monitor subjective areas of performance, such as the quality of internal and external content, by conducting 360-degree reviews or collecting data on the number of click-throughs for online posts.

Data can also help you understand how employees are optimizing their work: Are they working more overtime, cutting meetings, taking fewer breaks, working faster? You don't want people sacrificing breaks, rushing their work, or being on the clock longer, so if you see evidence of these behaviors, you might need to have conversations about reducing individual workloads or finding ways to make the work itself more efficient.

Most importantly, there is no need to reinvent the analysis wheel. While the specifics will be unique to your organization, there are numerous white papers, reports, and case studies you can look to for inspiration when making sense of your results. It can also be beneficial to partner with an academic or other specialist who can help you identify the most useful metrics and crunch the numbers.

Step 6: Scale Up—but Don't Stop Iterating

After you've evaluated the pilot and addressed any issues that emerged, take steps to make the schedule change permanent. Leaders will need to work across the organization to embed new practices into their workplace culture, ensure that people don't slip into old habits (no emailing on days off!), and remain focused on productivity—not hours worked—as the metric of success.

At the same time, it's critical to track success metrics over the long term and to adapt your processes according to what they show. One effective strategy is to maintain employee-led working sessions and focus groups even after the initial pilot results are analyzed, to help identify and overcome ongoing challenges. For example, after rolling out a four-day workweek, one company Charlotte worked with discovered that employees were suffering from a challenge known as the mere urgency effect: They became overly focused on urgent but less important tasks at the cost of long-term, more important ones. Based on this insight, the company scheduled monthly meetings to discuss long-term strategic plans, helping to keep priorities aligned.

The company also found that existing incentive structures were not as effective with the new working schedule. Specifically, sales teams, which were rewarded based on the number of deals closed, began prioritizing smaller accounts in order to close more deals in less time, rather than focusing on larger, strategically important accounts. As a result, the company reorganized the sales teams into dedicated small and large account specialists to ensure that equal resources would be spent on both areas of the business.

Of course, it's not just about productivity. Another company Charlotte worked with found that employees had begun working 10-hour days to fit work into a four-day week, significantly impacting job satisfaction and well-being. To address this, the leadership team restructured some divisions to make sure employees were focused on the right tasks, created new positions to focus on tasks outside the scope of existing teams, and used temporary contracts to ease the burden on full-time employees during rush periods.

Every organization will uncover its own challenges when it comes to scaling up a reduced work hours policy. Constant experimentation and iteration will be essential to any successful long-term rollout.

———————

Workplace norms have fundamentally shifted over the last year and a half. Today we find ourselves in a liminal period: We now have the chance to remake our models of work before things go back to the way they were—and that's an opportunity leaders must not squander. While no change comes easily, leaders willing to embrace models like the four-day workweek will find the experimentation well worth the effort.

Originally published in September 2018. Reprint H06L8C

Eliminate Strategic Overload

by Felix Oberholzer-Gee

IN THE PAST FEW DECADES, strategy has become increasingly sophisticated and complicated. If you work for a sizable organization, chances are your company has a marketing strategy (to track and shape consumer tastes), a corporate strategy (to benefit from synergies), a global strategy (to capture worldwide business opportunities), an innovation strategy (to pull ahead of the competition), a digital strategy (to exploit the internet), and a social strategy (to interact with communities online). In each of those domains, talented people work on a long list of urgent initiatives.

Companies are right, of course, to consider all these challenges. Rapid technological change, global competition, and ever-evolving consumer tastes—to name just a few of the pressures companies confront—all conspire to upend traditional ways of doing business. By responding to each of the new challenges, we ask ever more of our organizations and place ever-higher expectations on our employees. When I visit companies to do research and write cases, I am astonished by how much people accomplish in short periods of time with limited resources—but also very concerned about their long work hours and seemingly impossible stretch goals.

With alarming frequency, all these well-intentioned initiatives don't add up to corporate success. Take firm profitability as one example: A quarter of the firms in the S&P 500 earn long-term returns below their cost of capital. How can it be that so many companies, their ranks filled with talented and highly engaged employees, have so little to show for so much effort? Why do hard work and sophisticated strategy lead to enduring financial success for some companies but not for others?

I believe that strategic management faces an attractive, back-to-basics opportunity. By simplifying strategy—by selecting fewer initiatives with greater impact—we can make it more powerful. In this article, I describe an easy-to-use framework called value-based strategy, which gives executives a common language for evaluating strategic initiatives and developing a holistic view of the many activities taking place within their organizations.

The Elements of Value-Based Strategy

There's a simple principle at the heart of this approach: Companies that achieve enduring financial success create substantial value for their customers, their employees, and their suppliers. Therefore, a strategic initiative is worthwhile only if it does one of the following:

Creates value for customers by raising their willingness to pay (WTP)

If companies find ways to innovate or to improve existing products, people will be willing to pay more. In many product categories, Apple gets to charge a price premium because the company raises the customers' WTP by designing beautiful products that are easy to use, for example. Gucci increases customers' WTP by creating products that confer social status. In casual conversations, we often use WTP and price interchangeably. But it is helpful to distinguish between the two. WTP is the most a customer would ever be willing to pay. Think of it as the customer's walk-away point: Charge one cent more than someone's WTP, and that person is better off not buying.

Too often, managers focus on top-line growth rather than on increasing willingness to pay. A growth-focused manager asks, "What will help me sell more?" A person concerned with WTP wants to make her customers clap and cheer. A sales-centric manager analyzes purchase decisions and hopes to sway customers, whereas a value-focused manager searches for ways to increase WTP at every

Idea in Brief

The Problem

As companies respond to intensifying competitive pressures and challenges, they ask more and more of their employees. But organizations often have very little to show for the often Herculean efforts of their talented and engaged workers.

The Approach

Leaders can address this problem by simplifying strategy—that is, selecting fewer initiatives with greater impact. A value-based strategy gives executives a holistic view of the many activities taking place within their organizations.

The Process

A strategic initiative is worthwhile only if it does one or more of the following: creates value for customers by raising their willingness to pay, creates value for employees by making work more appealing, or creates value for suppliers by reducing their operating cost.

stage of the customer's journey, earning the customer's trust and loyalty. A value-focused company convinces its customers in every interaction that it has their best interests at heart.

Creates value for employees by making work more appealing

When companies make work more interesting, motivating, and flexible, they are able to attract talent even if they do not offer industry-leading compensation. Paying employees more is often the right thing to do, of course. But keep in mind that more-generous compensation does not create value in and of itself; it simply shifts resources from the business to the workforce. By contrast, offering better jobs not only creates value, it also lowers the minimum compensation that you have to offer to attract talent to your business, or what we call an employee's willingness-to-sell (WTS) wage. Offer a prospective employee even a little less than her WTS, and she will reject your job offer; she is better off staying with her current firm. As is the case with prices and WTP, value-focused organizations never confuse compensation and WTS.

Value-focused businesses think holistically about the needs of their employees (or the factors that drive WTS). When the Gap learned that one of retail workers' biggest problems was the lack of predictable and personalized schedules, it experimented with standardizing the start and end times of work shifts and scheduled employees for the same shift every day. In addition, Shift Messenger, an innovative app created specifically for the multistore experiment, allowed workers to trade shifts freely. During a 10-month test period, labor productivity went up 6.8% and sales rose nearly $3 million in participating stores. By creating value for its workers, the Gap increased employee well-being—workers even reported better sleep quality—and the company's financial performance improved.

Creates value for suppliers by reducing their operating cost

Like employees, suppliers expect a minimum level of compensation for their product. A company creates value for its suppliers by helping them raise their productivity. As suppliers' costs go down, the lowest price they would be willing to accept for their goods—what we call their willingness-to-sell (WTS) price—falls. When Nike, for example, created a training center in Sri Lanka to teach its Asian suppliers lean manufacturing, the improved production techniques helped suppliers reap better profits, which they then shared with Nike.

Value-focused executives evaluate every strategic move, every idea that comes across their desk, through the lens of value creation. Unless an initiative creates value for customers, employees, or suppliers— unless it moves the needle on WTP or WTS—it's not worth doing.

This idea is captured in a simple graph, called a value stick. WTP sits at the top and WTS at the bottom. When companies find ways to increase customer delight and increase employee satisfaction and supplier surplus (the difference between the price of goods and the lowest amount the supplier would be willing to accept for them), they expand the total amount of value created and position themselves for extraordinary financial performance. (See the exhibit "The value creation opportunity.")

Value-Based Strategy in Action

The strategic insight is simple; implementing it requires discipline. In my research work with organizations that exemplify value-based strategy, I've observed some key patterns.

FIGURE 2-1

The value creation opportunity

When companies find ways to increase customer delight, employee satisfaction, and supplier surplus, they expand the total amount of value they create and position themselves for extraordinary financial performance.

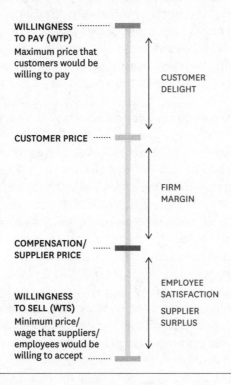

WILLINGNESS TO PAY (WTP)
Maximum price that customers would be willing to pay

CUSTOMER DELIGHT

CUSTOMER PRICE

FIRM MARGIN

COMPENSATION/ SUPPLIER PRICE

WILLINGNESS TO SELL (WTS)
Minimum price/ wage that suppliers/ employees would be willing to accept

EMPLOYEE SATISFACTION

SUPPLIER SURPLUS

They focus on value, not profit

Perhaps surprisingly, value-focused managers are not overly concerned with the immediate financial consequences of their decisions. They are confident that superior value creation will result in improved financial performance over time.

By contrast, companies obsessed with short-term returns often undermine value creation. In 1997, Excite, one of the original internet portals, declined to purchase the search technology that ultimately became Google for a paltry $1.6 million because it was *too good*. Excite's business model depended on advertising. The longer users spent on its site, and the more often they returned, the more money the company would make. In Excite's world, it was a terrible idea to quickly send users elsewhere by providing highly relevant search results. To optimize profitability, the company thought, it was best to have a search engine that was about 80% as good as other engines. Had its executives been thinking about value for their customers rather than their own bottom line, they would have made a different—and ultimately far more profitable—decision.

They attract the employees and customers whom they serve best
As companies find ways to move WTP or WTS, they make themselves more appealing to customers and employees who particularly like how they add value. Uber has twice the share of female drivers that taxi companies have because it made the job safer, increasing satisfaction for those drivers in particular. Florida's BayCare health organization is nationally recognized for the quality of its training programs. Not surprisingly, it is an attractive employer for health care professionals who value continuing education.

Similar dynamics play out in competition for customers. South Africa's Discovery insurance company creates value by offering an entire suite of health-improving services, including access to fitness clubs, health wearables, and even incentives to buy healthful foods in supermarkets. Predictably, individuals who are especially health conscious find Discovery's policies extra appealing.

It is an unfair advantage, really. Value-focused companies get to serve the very customers who like their products best, they attract talent that values the organization's strategy and culture, and they boost corporate performance.

They create value for customers, employees, or suppliers (or some combination) simultaneously
Traditional thinking, informed by our early understanding of success in manufacturing, holds that costs for companies will rise if

FIGURE 2-2

Best Buy's value-based strategy

In response to increased competitive pressure from online and low-cost rivals, Best Buy transformed its physical stores from a liability to an asset. It invited suppliers to develop stores-within-the-store, raising willingness to pay and greatly increasing value for customers, vendors, and employees.

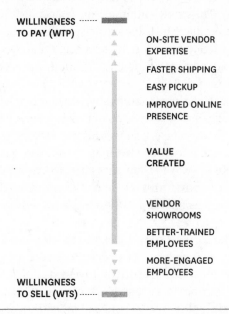

they boost consumers' willingness to pay—that is, it takes more-costly inputs to create a better product. But value-focused organizations find ways to defy that logic.

Best Buy, circa 2012, illustrates the point. Amazon was threatening the big-box giant by offering consumers a broad selection of products, aggressively priced. Walmart and other brick-and-mortar competitors were stealing market share by focusing on the most popular electronic devices and selling high volumes of them at low prices. Consumers had started to "showroom," visiting stores to decide what they liked and then buying products elsewhere online.

In response, Hubert Joly, Best Buy's new CEO, led a far-ranging strategic and operational overhaul. Rather than thinking of Best Buy's more than 1,000 stores as liabilities, the company turned them into assets. They invited suppliers to create stores-within-the-store as a way to draw customers in and hold on to them. Apple, Samsung, Sony, and eventually even Amazon signed on, investing hundreds of millions of dollars in Best Buy's stores and subsidizing the company's employees. The stores-within-a-store concept allowed Best Buy to offer deeper product and sales expertise (raising customers' WTP) and also benefited the vendors by lowering their operating costs, thus increasing supplier surplus. In addition, the retailer started using the stores as distribution centers, which allowed it to beat Amazon on shipping times. And finally, the initiative changed how managers thought about Best Buy's online presence. The company had long seen its website as a substitute, threatening the core business, and so it had underinvested in it. Now the company reimagined the website as a way to allow customers to explore their options before coming to a physical store—and invested in building a strong online presence. (See the exhibit "Best Buy's value-based strategy.")

The turnaround provided Best Buy with a new lease on life. As is typical for value-focused companies, the retailer found many ways to simultaneously increase WTP and WTS. Predictably, profits followed. By 2016, Best Buy's return on invested capital had climbed from negative territory to 23%, and its pretax margins had doubled.

Additional examples, from a variety of industries, abound. When Quest Diagnostics created more-attractive work conditions for its call center employees, attrition dropped, unplanned absences fell, and the percentage of calls answered within 60 seconds rose. In other words, employee-related costs went down (even though opportunities to make more money through exceptional performance increased) and the value created went up. Because of the improved service quality, Quest customers' willingness to pay went up at the same time. Zara's fast-fashion model reduces inventory (lowering suppliers' required working capital and increasing their surplus) and provides customers with the latest trends in cuts and color (increasing their WTP). Progressive's fleet of emergency vehicles allows the insurer to take better care of customers who have had an accident, increasing WTP, and it lowers fraud and administrative expenses, reducing costs and WTS.

They pursue complements as a rich source of value creation
Value-based organizations are good at spotting complements, or products and services that enhance the value of their core offering. Complements are a familiar feature of the strategy landscape—think printers and cartridges, coffee machines and capsules, tablets and e-books. But at the outset, they can be difficult to identify. When I ask students what would complement a movie theater's offering, they think of popcorn and Coke, advance ticket sales, and more-comfortable seats. They rarely suggest childcare services—but that's what Harkins Theatres, an Arizona-based chain of movie theaters, offers its patrons. It staffs its play centers with trained professionals who look after children while their parents watch a movie, pager in hand to inform them if problems arise. As this example illustrates, complements often seem unrelated to the core business. Identifying them requires you to think creatively about customer journeys.

Even if a new offering is quite obviously a complement to an existing business, keeping a close eye on the customer's journey can uncover new ways to use it to create customer value. Amazon beat Sony on e-readers even though it was late to the market, had no technology advantage, and was working with a more limited marketing budget. How? Wireless access. The Kindle's free 3G internet access made books an impulse purchase and turned out to be of huge value to customers—and thus to Amazon.

Complements raise customers' willingness to pay for the core product, whereas substitutes have the opposite effect—so you might think that it's easy to distinguish between the two. But this is true only in hindsight. Personal computers were supposed to be a substitute for paper. (Remember the paperless office?) They turned out to be a complement: As personal computers became ubiquitous, the demand for paper exploded. ATMs were thought to eliminate bank teller positions. They didn't. Digital music formats proved to be a substitute for CDs—but a complement for live concerts. Across many examples and industries, business history reveals a clear pattern: Companies often mistake complements for substitutes.

FIGURE 2-3

Apple's shifting profit pool

As competition in hardware intensified, it became tougher for Apple to earn a higher WTP on its devices, so it shifted its profit pool to software, increasing gross margins in its app store fourfold from 2009 to 2019. (Calculating Apple's margins is tricky, but detective work by analysts Horace Dediu and Kulbinder Garcha reveals the dramatic shift.)

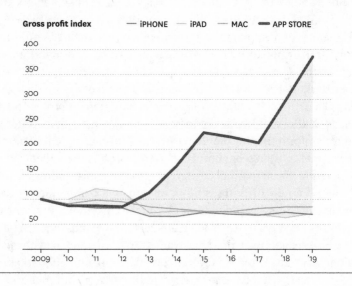

Value-focused organizations are better at spotting the true relationship between new technologies and legacy products because they are keenly aware of how customers benefit from technological changes. By contrast, companies that focus on sales growth and monetization see most advances as threats to their business models. They habitually take a defensive stance, missing important opportunities to create value in novel ways.

They shift profit pools to capture value over time

Traditionally strategists have differentiated between value creation (the topic of this article for the most part) and value capture (how to make money from the value you've created). Value-focused businesses concentrate on the former, but they tend to be flexible about the latter. Because they take a broad view of customer needs, they frequently offer solutions that go beyond their core products. These product-and-service bundles enhance value capture opportunities because they allow businesses to shift their profit pools from one offering to another as the life cycle of the product—or the market overall—changes.

Apple's mobile devices are a good example. Early in its history, the iPhone was clearly differentiated from competing products and provided substantial value for its customers. Apple later created services like iTunes, but it barely monetized them. Keeping the price of complements low, the company understood, further increased the appeal of Apple hardware. More recently, however, it is harder to argue that customer WTP for Apple's devices is far higher than the WTP for competing phones. How did Apple respond to the increased competition? It shifted the profit pool from hardware to services (or apps), the segment where its competitive standing is barely contested. (See the exhibit "Apple's shifting profit pool.")

Shifts in profit pools are not unique to Apple. Amazon subsidizes the Kindle to boost the WTP for e-books. Microsoft shifts profits from its game console to the games. The Indian ride-sharing company Ola created an entire suite of payment options (including Hospicash, an innovative offering that covers travel to hospitals and postdischarge expenditures) that contribute to Ola's strategic flexibility. Two patterns are noteworthy. First, businesses tend to shift profit pools away from hotly contested markets to segments where it is easier to defend high margins. Second, the financial consequences of these shifts are particularly favorable if the products are complements: As the price of one product declines, WTP (and value capture opportunities) for the complement increases.

Getting Started

WTP and WTS sit at the core of value-based strategy, but because the concepts are quite abstract, it can be challenging to see how to bring

FIGURE 2-4

Tatra's customer value maps

As these value maps demonstrate, Tatra banka's value proposition is better aligned with the preferences of premium customers than its competitors'. It has more room for improvement with its mass-market customers.

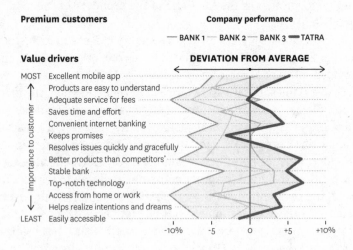

Premium customers

Company performance

— BANK 1 — BANK 2 — BANK 3 ▬ TATRA

Value drivers

DEVIATION FROM AVERAGE

Importance to customer

MOST
Excellent mobile app
Products are easy to understand
Adequate service for fees
Saves time and effort
Convenient internet banking
Keeps promises
Resolves issues quickly and gracefully
Better products than competitors'
Stable bank
Top-notch technology
Access from home or work
Helps realize intentions and dreams
LEAST Easily accessible

-10%   -5   0   +5   +10%

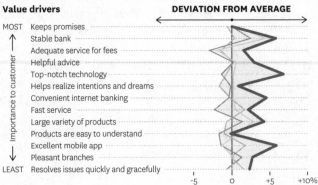

Mass-market customers

Value drivers

DEVIATION FROM AVERAGE

Importance to customer

MOST
Keeps promises
Stable bank
Adequate service for fees
Helpful advice
Top-notch technology
Helps realize intentions and dreams
Convenient internet banking
Fast service
Large variety of products
Products are easy to understand
Excellent mobile app
Pleasant branches
LEAST Resolves issues quickly and gracefully

-5   0   +5   +10%

Source: Tatra banka and Kantar Slovakia

them to life in your organization. At Harvard Business School, we often use a visualization tool called the value map to help executives identify strategic opportunities. It's proven helpful for anything from a half-day examination of a particular business to a full-bore strategy overhaul, and it's useful for testing the tenets of value-based strategy against whatever's happening in your company.

You begin by selecting a group of customers: your most profitable segment, perhaps. Next you compile a list of criteria that are important to those customers when they make a purchase. These criteria are called value drivers. Think of them as the product and service attributes that determine WTP. You then rank the value drivers from most to least important from the customers' point of view. In a final step, you determine for each driver how good your company is at meeting customers' expectations and do the same for your major competitors.

It's important not to make assumptions about what your customers value most and how well you deliver. If you're going to reformulate your strategy on the basis of your value map, you need good data to assist you in building it. When I see companies undertake a serious value-map analysis, there is almost always a surprise—a driver that turns out to be less critical than commonly thought or an unexpected level of performance on another dimension. These surprises aside, I find that most companies have a fairly accurate sense about their own performance but tend to know far less about how their customers view the performance of their competitors. That too requires research and data gathering.

Consider the two value maps for Tatra banka, Slovakia's first post-communist private bank. Founded in 1990, Tatra quickly led European banking in the adoption of digital technology. It first offered mobile banking in 2009 and introduced voice biometrics in 2013 and facial recognition in 2018, earning more than 100 awards for its innovative services. As I worked with Tatra to develop its strategy, the bank collected data from customers through surveys and interviews and used it to create value maps for premium and mass-market customers. Looking at the maps, it is evident why Tatra had particular success with the former segment: Excellent mobile technology is what premium customers value most, and the bank led its competitors on that measure. Mass-market customers, by contrast, were most concerned with whether the bank kept its promises, one of the areas where Tatra did not stand out. (See the exhibit "Tatra's customer value maps.")

Value drivers can serve as innovation engines because they live midway between the rather abstract notion of WTP and WTS and the very specific attributes that describe your current product or service. This has two advantages. First, value drivers are useful for analyzing the existing business. It's a straightforward task to link a given value driver to operating models and KPIs and to compare performance with that of competitors. Second, they can be helpful in thinking about opportunities, because they don't specify in any detail how you will meet a particular customer need. They help you explore new ways to satisfy customers, employees, and suppliers. Focusing on value drivers, rather than patterns of past success or industry trends, you are less likely to equate business success with selling more of what you already offer. (See the exhibit "Value maps for employees and suppliers.")

Once you've created the map, it's time to identify the drivers that offer the most potential for future value creation and to think through strategic initiatives that will support them. That work is too nuanced and company-specific to do justice to here (a fuller description is available in my book *Better, Simpler Strategy*), but keep these three principles in mind.

Invest in a small number of related value drivers

Choosing how to improve your company's value proposition is ultimately a question of forecasting the return on various investment opportunities. How much does it cost to move a particular value driver, and what increase in WTP can you expect in return? Many companies find it beneficial to identify a cluster of related value drivers that add up to a bigger theme. This helps them stand out in the minds of their customers ("Tatra is the technology leader in banking"), and it is operationally efficient because closely related

FIGURE 2-5

Value maps for employees and suppliers

Value maps also provide a deep understanding of employee or supplier willingness to sell. Here we see that Tatra lags competing employers in satisfying the value drivers that matter most to tellers.

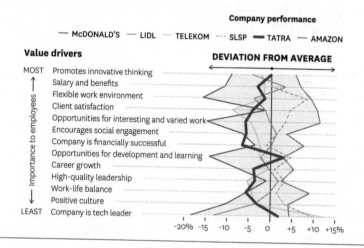

drivers are often supported by similar activities. For instance, building digital capabilities allowed Tatra to improve on several important value drivers.

Resist the temptation to play catch-up

When executives first study their value maps, many concentrate on drivers where their company lags, and they quickly identify initiatives that would allow them to catch up with the competition. This is a mistake. The ability to capture value depends on differences in value creation. When a customer is choosing between two companies with nearly identical value maps, her attention will go to price. The greater the similarity between two companies' value maps, the greater the pressure to compete on price. The goal is to increase differentiation, not to close gaps.

Insist on making trade-offs

When I work on value maps with executives, they understand in the abstract that all companies need to choose where to focus their energy and resources. But when they examine their own value maps, they want to bring every value driver up to the maximum rating. I see this so often that I know it's a powerful impulse—but it needs to be quashed, because a strong strategy always involves trade-offs. No company can be good at everything.

Creating value for customers, employees, and suppliers sits at the very heart of strategies that result in stellar performance. In the best companies, this orientation toward value creation is reflected in every decision made by employees at all levels of the organization. The focus on creating value shows up in big strategic plans and in small everyday choices.

A few years ago, I had an interaction with a salesperson at a flower shop that illustrates how a focus on value creation can permeate an entire organization, even in the briefest of customer interactions. I had meant to send flowers to a friend for her birthday, but her day came and went and somehow I forgot. A few days later, I remembered and called the shop to place an order. It was late afternoon, and the salesperson asked whether I wanted to have the flowers delivered that day or the next. I confessed to being late for my friend's birthday and urged the salesperson to send them as quickly as possible. Her response caught me by surprise. "Shall we take the blame for the late delivery?" she asked.

I didn't want her to lie for me, of course, so I didn't take her up on the offer. But even in that brief conversation, I recognized that this salesperson didn't see her job as simply selling flowers. Rather, she was focused on creating value for her customers by increasing their WTP—which she did. The following year, I received an email from the flower shop a few days before my friend's birthday, reminding me it was time to place an order. I did so, at what seemed to me an inflated price. But I was willing to pay it as a fair trade for the shop's solving my problem—a win for the flower shop's strategy.

Originally published in May–June 2021. Reprint R2103E

Drive Innovation with Better Decision-Making

by Linda A. Hill, Emily Tedards, and Taran Swan

TO STAY COMPETITIVE, TODAY'S BUSINESS leaders are investing millions in digital tools, agile methodologies, and lean strategies.

Too often, however, those efforts produce neither the breakthrough operational processes nor the blockbuster business models companies need—at least not before their competitors introduce their own advances. And a key culprit is the inability to make quick and effective innovation decisions.

The discovery-driven innovation processes companies now rely on involve an unprecedented number of choices, from big go/no-go gates that govern which ideas are pursued to countless decisions about how to conduct experiments, what data to collect, how to interpret findings, and how to act on them. But in companies that are just learning to experiment, too many decisions are made inefficiently or informed by past experience and narrow perspectives. As a result, critical risks aren't identified, and bad ideas hang around forever, eating up scarce resources and crushing the chances of bigger, more-transformative bets.

Take Pfizer. (One of us, Hill, has been a paid adviser to the company over the years.) In 2015 the pharmaceutical giant kicked off a digital transformation effort in its Global Clinical Supply (GCS) arm, which delivers more than a million doses of investigative medicines to thousands of clinical sites in over 70 countries each year. Doing so while maintaining clinical trial integrity is a complex task. Any issue, such as inadequate refrigeration, unclear instructions for medical professionals, or patients' failure to comply with regimens, could delay the development of potentially lifesaving treatments. By 2018, GCS had made significant progress with its digital initiatives. But with new medical and digital technologies on the horizon, Pfizer's strategy changed to focus exclusively on breakthrough drugs and vaccines. GCS needed to become ever more agile, innovative, and patient focused so that it could adapt to myriad clinical-site and patient needs. Findings from a cultural survey, however, underscored that the organization was struggling to make good, timely decisions about systems, processes, and capability innovations.

So GCS altered its approach on a number of fronts, creating cross-functional teams that were responsible for key decisions, changing the frequency of decision-making meetings, and improving team members' ability to robustly debate ideas. Those efforts paid off when Covid hit: Thanks in no small part to the quick-footed support of GCS, the first emergency authorization of the Pfizer-BioNTech vaccine was granted only 266 days after the declaration of the pandemic. (GCS's journey in advance of the pandemic will be described throughout this article; for more on the race to make the vaccine, see "The CEO of Pfizer on Developing a Vaccine in Record Time," HBR, May–June 2021.) GCS's success at rapidly delivering tens of thousands of doses of the vaccine candidates and collaborating with colleagues across Pfizer to develop solutions to the thorny challenge of preserving them at subzero temperatures is just the most prominent of its many recent innovation achievements, which range from real-time tracking of trial-drug shipments to personalized tests for cutting-edge therapies.

We've spent almost two decades studying leaders at highly innovative organizations and, more recently, incumbent firms that are on their way to becoming innovation powerhouses. When we looked closely at 65 of the companies that were on the journey to becoming more nimble, we found that the more successful ones were applying many agile and lean principles to decision-making itself. In this

Idea In Brief

The Problem

Despite their embrace of agile and lean methodologies, many organizations looking to become more innovative are still struggling to move quickly on new ideas. That's often because of their outdated, inefficient approach to decision-making.

The Research

Over the past two decades the authors have worked with innovative companies across the globe, most recently focusing on incumbent firms that were transforming themselves into nimbler businesses, to learn what key challenges they faced and how they addressed them.

The Solution

Businesses need to strengthen and speed up their creative decision-making processes by including diverse perspectives, clarifying decision rights, matching the cadence of decisions to the pace of learning, and encouraging candid, robust conflict in service of a better experience for the end customer. Only then will all that rapid experimentation pay off.

article we'll show what that means: including diverse perspectives, clarifying decision rights, matching the cadence of decision-making to the pace of learning, and encouraging candid, healthy conflict in service of a better experience for the end customer.

Diverse Perspectives

Research has long shown that diverse teams are better at identifying opportunities and risks in any problem-solving situation. But in organizations that are learning to experiment, four perspectives tend to be underrepresented in decision-making:

The customer perspective

It's hardly a surprise that the customer needs to be at the heart of all decisions, whether they're about new products, business models, or internal processes. But we find that customer intimacy is all too rare. Because of that, firms end up chasing problems that don't really matter to customers and miss opportunities to address their unarticulated pain points and desires.

How to Avoid Common Traps

A NUMBER OF TRADITIONAL decision-making habits can hinder agile decision-making. They need to be unlearned.

Don't let leaders and experts dominate.

More often than not, at the end of decision-making processes, one individual confidently makes the final call. This frequently stems from something innocuous: a respect for expertise. The problem is, experts can quickly become naysayers who shut down conversation. That's dangerous since they're often the most wedded to the status quo. Imagine a team with one digital expert who dismisses others' ideas about technology as naive or infeasible. No one wants to look ill-informed, so team members are likely to keep silent.

To combat this, experts should be asked to provide evidence for their points of view just like everyone else, keeping the argument rooted in fact rather than opinion or politics. Some leaders remove themselves from the process once the problem has been framed, letting their teams make the ultimate choice. Leaders often tell us it can be hard to stay quiet; Jessie Woolley-Wilson, the CEO of the ed-tech company DreamBox Learning, admits, "I am the worst practitioner of that because I get so excited and want to bring energy to the discussion." But she reminds herself, "My goal is to make fewer and fewer decisions."

Don't let people go along to get along.

Compromise to avoid conflict can be superficial—everyone agrees while in the room but disagrees after leaving it—and it usually prioritizes employees' needs over customer experience. A good way to avoid this problem is to have proponents of each alternative make the case for other options. That helps all involved broaden their points of view, empathize with the logic of their

The solution here is to include in your decision-making processes the people who are most closely connected with end customers: frontline operations staff, customer service employees, salespeople, and the customers themselves. Organizations that are good at this also tend to work closely with user experience or user interface teams, ethnographic researchers, or experts in human-centric design. And if you're developing a new business process or a digital tool for employees, remember that *their* voices need to be heard—in this case they are the customers who will use it.

teammates, and make sure they really understand an idea before discarding it. People should be encouraged to ask questions like "What am I not seeing?" and "Where is my expertise creating blind spots?" and open-ended "what-if" questions to help them let go of any assumptions constraining their thinking.

Avoiding compromise can lead to novel solutions. In one company we studied, the marketing and product divisions were deadlocked over a new service that the product team envisioned offering through the company's mobile app. The marketing division believed it wouldn't bring in a large-enough return to justify the costs of adding it to the app. The service went nowhere for nearly three years, until the company brought in a new innovation leader who asked, "What if we promoted the service somewhere other than the app?" The ultimate solution this prompted was neither a compromise nor one of the two original options: The team developed the service and touted it over SMS and email. Ultimately, its success provided the data the marketing team needed to confidently add the feature to the mobile app.

Don't let people make a decision prematurely.

Decision-makers trying to keep up with the pace of change typically lean toward urgency. But even in an agile framework, the leader's role is to sense when more learning or synthesis of ideas is necessary and encourage patience.

At P&G, when a team wants to scale up a new product idea, its executive sponsor requires evidence that the product offers an "irresistibly superior experience" to customers. If the results look promising but not compelling enough to support a launch, teams are encouraged to continue to incubate the idea. Running additional experiments and collecting more data often leads to pivots that increase the value proposition.

To represent the voices of patients in clinical trials and the health care professionals working directly with them, Pfizer's GCS unit created a new function, Clinical Research Pharmacy, and recruited pharmacists (who had prior experience administering the treatments) to join it. Over time, the CRP came to play an integral role in decision-making at GCS. Its pharmacists' insights have led to innovations ranging from user-friendly package designs to virtual-reality training for health care providers.

The local perspective

Too often decisions in global companies are made at headquarters without adequately taking into account perspectives from different geographies. Yet people at headquarters rarely have the contextual intelligence required to judge which new business models, services, or operations are best suited to a local economy and regulatory environment. Getting local input can make a big difference.

At GCS, strategic decisions, even those that affected regional operations, had been made principally by U.S. teams. But once the unit began deliberately soliciting ideas from local managers, empowering them to innovate, it saw impressive improvements. For instance, when a new Latin America–based team was established, it used its expertise to cut the time it took to get trial medicines to local health care providers and patients from 55 to 20 days.

Even more prevalent is the failure to transfer local insights back to a business's core processes and products. Often small divisions in small markets can be quicker and more innovative than their larger counterparts in home markets. For example, eBay's successful Buy It Now button, which revolutionized e-commerce and helped shopping move online, was developed by eBay Germany and was based on its deep relationships with its user communities.

The data-informed perspective

Especially in years like the past one, when the business environment was in constant flux, relying on past experience to guide innovation efforts may lead a company astray. Lean methods call for testing ideas and using near-real-time quantitative and qualitative data to decide next steps. The challenge lies in making that information accessible to every decision-maker.

Data visualization provides a solution: It can allow timely, complex information to be interpreted by people from a variety of functional backgrounds, leveling the playing field so that those who are less data savvy can fully engage when making decisions.

At GCS, a new digital-business-operations group created visual dashboards that superimposed information about events such as weather, flight, and shipping route disruptions over supply chain data to predict risks to operations in real time. These dashboards, which were accessible to all team members, proved invaluable at the daily "light speed" meetings held to respond to the Covid crisis as it upended supply chains, shut down borders, and overwhelmed the hospitals running Pfizer's clinical trials. GCS teams were able to make critical decisions about the processes for supplying ongoing trials across the globe, including those for the new Covid vaccine candidates and antivirals. Despite the logistical challenges brought on by the pandemic and natural disasters from wildfires to hurricanes, the organization didn't miss a single delivery to trial patients.

The outside perspective

Even the best-intentioned innovators can get mired in their companies' dominant logic. Leaders of incumbent firms, especially ones that are still growing, albeit slowly, tend to reject bold ideas—ideas that present high risk as well as high reward, require new resources or capabilities, or threaten to cannibalize the core business. An outside view can help organizations contemplate those moves more seriously.

That outside view can come from within the company, however. GCS invited high-potential talent from other parts of Pfizer to join its leadership team permanently, increasing the group from six to 16 members. Many leaders at other firms ask less experienced, recently hired employees to attend C-suite meetings. Because these people aren't steeped in the company's inner workings, they ask questions that challenge core assumptions and help reframe strategic choices.

An outside perspective can also come from beyond the company's walls or even its industry. GCS, for example, invited people from Delta Air Lines' innovation lab to participate in a design workshop on the clinical trial experience for patients. Delta's boarding-pass scanner and bag-tracking capabilities sparked ideas for new ways that GCS could enhance its own shipment-tracking capabilities, ensuring that more patients got the right dose of the right drug at the right time.

Clear Decision Rights

As they recognize the need to bring together many points of view, a lot of organizations are relying more on decentralized networks of cross-functional teams, both permanent and ad hoc, to increase their agility. But this can have a downside: Involving more voices in a decision can mean less clarity about who ultimately owns it, slowing the innovation process and often prompting frustration and disengagement.

For example, when executives at a financial services firm asked their high-potential team leaders to identify and pursue new business models, the results were disappointing. The team leaders didn't understand that they'd been given the authority to make decisions themselves and often came back to the executives and suggested options to choose from, rather than proposing an intended plan of action. The team leaders also had a mixed experience. At first they were honored and energized by being selected for an innovative project. But later they became discouraged by the disconnect between their recommendations and the decisions of the executives—who'd fallen back into their habit of calling the shots—and ultimately, by the ambiguity about decision-making rights.

To effectively empower decision-makers, leaders must be explicit in every case about who will be *responsible* for executing the decision, who will be *accountable* for making it, who will be *consulted*, and who will be *informed*. (Creating and sharing a traditional RACI chart can do the trick here.) If leaders are delegating decisions to a group, they should specify the process to be used and the parameters of the group's authority for everyone involved.

GCS transferred ownership of the investigative drug supply from a single leader to cross-functional teams of four known as "tetrads." Each tetrad became responsible for one therapeutic area. The members were collectively accountable for decisions, and they had clear guidelines about when they should escalate a decision to the tetrad's executive sponsors. It took some months for everyone involved to feel confident about the new structure and to refine the guidelines, but ultimately the tetrads helped GCS kill less promising ideas faster, without having to push those choices up to senior leadership.

With their enterprisewide view, the teams were also able to begin proposing more-innovative ideas for optimizing the whole clinical supply chain, such as how to pioneer delivery of highly personalized gene-therapy drugs.

The Right Cadence

Established companies tend to make innovation decisions on a fixed schedule, through quarterly or annual reviews at which senior teams step back, assess past plans, and make new ones. But in agile companies, innovation is based on discovery-driven learning. With each experiment, data and insights emerge that should be taken into consideration in setting up the next one. Leaders must encourage decisions to be made at a pace aligned with the learning cycle.

To gauge the right cadence for your meetings, think about how long it will take to gather enough data to validate (or disprove) your hypotheses. If you're learning quickly or confronting rapid change, you may need to make decisions more frequently. During the pandemic, for example, most leadership teams at companies we observed naturally increased the cadence of meetings. Given the unfolding nature of the crisis, every decision had to be considered a "working hypothesis," so they opted for short sessions daily over longer ones every few weeks. Many told us they hope to stick with the new, faster rhythm even after the pandemic is over.

The many decisions that come up daily in experimentation often call for continuous processes. For example, in one Indian organization we studied, the design team created a WhatsApp forum to collect rapid feedback on its proposals from the whole organization, including remote employees working closely with end users in the field. Because the channel was always available, designers could spontaneously solicit feedback from employees and apply it to decisions immediately.

But longer timelines can still be needed to create the space necessary for collaboration and information gathering, especially if you're contemplating big bets. When Kathy Fish, P&G's former chief research, development, and innovation officer, introduced the lean startup model to her organization, the business units supplemented their annual planning processes with a review of innovation portfolios every 90 days in order to issue metered funding to the initiatives in them. That gave teams enough time to conduct experiments and consolidate findings while preserving their momentum.

Good Fights

Inviting diverse sets of participants to well-timed decision-making forums doesn't automatically lead to the thorough vetting of ideas. This is where so many organizations get stuck: They fail to create a competitive marketplace of ideas, where genuine debate increases the odds that risks are identified and the most-promising projects are pursued.

In some dysfunctional teams, productive discourse is stymied by political infighting, defensive behavior, or hidden agendas. Critiques of ideas often become critiques of personalities, and employees don't trust that their ideas will be taken seriously. Often any real conversations and decisions happen "outside the room," so members of the group feel disenfranchised even though they've been asked to participate.

Yet an even more common cause of unproductive debate is a culture of politeness. Many people try to minimize differences as opposed to amplifying them, in an effort to avoid conflict. The effect is that those with minority views don't speak up or compromise too quickly when they're challenged. As a result bosses or experts tend to dominate the decision-making process no matter how diverse the assembled group is.

In both kinds of situations, leaders must stop worrying about whether people can collaborate and instead worry about whether they know how to argue. Leaders can encourage the psychological safety that promotes good fights in three ways:

Ask questions
Leaders need to avoid shutting down the conversation with solutions from the outset. Instead, they should be transparent about what they don't know. At P&G (which has also hired Hill as an adviser in the past), leaders are encouraged to ask these four questions in response

to every experiment: *What did you learn? How do you know? What do you need to learn next? How can I help?* By demonstrating that they don't have all the answers, leaders help set the expectation that all present should share their opinions and that anyone can be wrong. They also create an environment in which people feel more comfortable challenging one another.

At Pfizer, team members were initially reluctant to disagree with vice president Michael Ku when he became the head of GCS. But as he learned to admit what he didn't know and adopted the habit of being the last person to share his thoughts in meetings, they became more comfortable speaking up.

Focus on the data

Data can provide a solid foundation for productive debate. Team members who have the same data visualizations in front of them are likelier to develop a shared understanding of problems—common ground on which they can add their unique perspectives. Ku ensured that all decisions made at GCS's monthly operational review were informed by data. When things had to move quickly during Covid, this kept the team from making choices based on emotion or past experiences that were no longer relevant.

Articulate a shared purpose

Aligning the whole organization around a common, meaningful purpose (why we exist and whom we serve) gives people permission to fight about new ideas, because they all agree about what they're fighting for. Ideally the purpose will serve as a framework that ensures that decisions benefit the end user or customer.

A shared ambition can keep debates from getting personal. At one retail company we studied, a team created avatars for key customer segments. "Ali" was the avatar for urban Millennials, for instance. Whenever a discussion started to get more personal than substantive, someone would intervene and ask, "What does Ali need from us all right now?" That encouraged the team to focus on a joint concern for customers instead of descending into a winner-takes-all argument.

FIGURE 3-1

Why focus on decision-making?

In our almost 20 years of research with organizations across the globe, we have identified the most important factors that support innovation—whether it's the invention of new product or service offerings, business processes or models, or ways of organizing or cutting costs. They include both cultural factors and capabilities.

All firms

Creative abrasion is the ability to generate a marketplace of ideas through discourse and debate.

Creative agility is the ability to do discovery-driven learning.

Creative resolution is the ability to make decisions that combine disparate and sometimes even opposing ideas.

Additional factors include decision-making basics, customer intimacy and innovation investment.

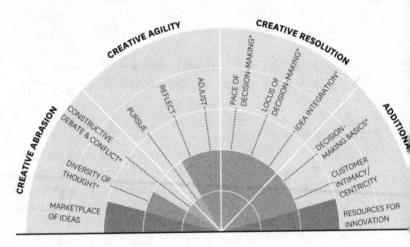

*Decision-making capabilities

A purpose can also encourage criticism rather than silent politeness. A real challenge in companies learning to be agile is killing "walking zombies"—projects without enough value to justify their continuation. To meet it, leaders should remind teams of their

In more-recent research, we've found that companies trying to become more innovative tend to do better at the cultural factors but have weaker capabilities, including decision-making.

Impact on innovation
Extent to which a
characteristic impedes or
facilitates innovation

IMPEDES   FACILITATES

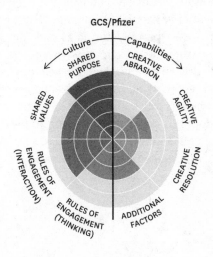

GCS/Pfizer

Culture — Capabilities

SHARED PURPOSE
CREATIVE ABRASION
CREATIVE AGILITY
SHARED VALUES
CREATIVE RESOLUTION
RULES OF ENGAGEMENT (INTERACTION)
RULES OF ENGAGEMENT (THINKING)
ADDITIONAL FACTORS

purpose. When Ku first took the reins at GCS, most people were reluctant to criticize others' ideas. Decision-makers interpreted silence as agreement that an idea was worth pursuing, so the number of projects underway became overwhelming. Ku's first priority was to align the entire team around a shared purpose: "Patients First." In debates about which initiatives to pursue, people learned to ask, "Is that the best solution for the patient?" rather than staying silent. The team soon found itself rejecting more ideas and able to focus more effort on those that enhanced the patient experience.

A common purpose helps decision-makers focus on solving problems rather than fulfilling personal agendas. In the midst of Covid, while everyone was working 24/7, Ku observed with pride that leaders in GCS were advocating for decisions that were in the best interests of the patient even when doing so meant more work for their own functional areas.

Leadership Matters

Organizations and teams must adopt new behaviors to make informed decisions more quickly, but managers need to change, too. Too many leaders act unilaterally, swooping in to save the day with the "right" answers—especially during a crisis. But when innovation is called for, leaders need to create environments in which their people can find answers on their own. It takes courage and practice to step back and let others make decisions and especially to avoid taking the bait when teams naturally try to delegate up the chain. But until you adopt this new way of working yourself, your organization will never be as innovative as it could be.

Originally published in November–December 2021. Reprint R2106D

Unconscious Bias Training That Works

by Francesca Gino and Katherine Coffman

ACROSS THE GLOBE, IN RESPONSE to public outcry over racist incidents in the workplace and mounting evidence of the cost of employees' feeling excluded, leaders are striving to make their companies more diverse, equitable, and inclusive. Unconscious bias training has played a major role in their efforts. UB training seeks to raise awareness of the mental shortcuts that lead to snap judgments—often based on race and gender—about people's talents or character. Its goal is to reduce bias in attitudes and behaviors at work, from hiring and promotion decisions to interactions with customers and colleagues.

But conventional UB training isn't working, research suggests. In a 2019 meta-analysis of more than 490 studies involving some 80,000 people, the psychologist Patrick Forscher and his colleagues found that UB training did not change biased behavior. Other studies have revealed that the training can backfire: Sending the message that biases are involuntary and widespread—beyond our control, in other words—can make people feel they're unavoidable and lead to more discrimination, not less. In fact, in a 2006 review of more than 700 companies, Alexandra Kalev, Frank Dobbin, and Erin Kelly showed that after UB training, the likelihood that Black men and women would advance in organizations often *decreased*. It's no wonder that women and people of color continue to report high levels of unfair treatment at work.

The most effective UB training does more than increase awareness of bias and its impact. It teaches attendees to manage their biases, change their behavior, and track their progress. It gives them information that contradicts stereotypes and allows them to connect with people whose experiences are different from theirs. And it's not just a onetime education session; it entails a longer journey and structural changes to policies and operations—like the standardization of hiring processes, the elimination of self-assessments from performance reviews, and the institution of incentives for improving diversity. Rather than providing UB training as a check-the-box exercise, companies make a real, long-term commitment to it because they think it's worthy and important.

In a study we conducted at a pharmaceutical company, the results of two surveys we did, and the work of other scholars, we see the positive impact this style of UB training has. Not only do employees report heightened awareness of bias, but they also *show* less bias and prejudice weeks after the training. They start finding the workplace to be more inclusive—somewhere that differences are cherished rather than tolerated. And women, people of color, and people with disabilities report feeling a greater sense of belonging and respect for their contributions.

To unpack what drives these positive changes, we interviewed dozens of leaders—including chief human resource officers, learning and development executives, and diversity, equity, and inclusion officers—at companies that have implemented rigorous UB programs across a variety of industries. In this article we'll share what we've learned about how they're leveraging a more practical approach to UB training. (Disclosure: One of us—Gino—has conducted antibias training at organizations as a consultant, but they include none of the companies featured in this article.)

The Flaws in Conventional Approaches

Traditional UB training falls short in a number of ways. In a recent survey we did of more than 500 working adults from a wide range of U.S. organizations, three findings stood out. First, most

Idea in Brief

The Problem

Conventional training to combat unconscious bias and make the workplace more diverse, equitable, and inclusive isn't working.

The Cause

This training aims to raise employees' awareness of biases based on race or gender. But by also sending the message that such biases are involuntary and widespread, it can make people feel that they're unavoidable.

The Solution

Companies must go beyond raising awareness and teach people to manage biases and change behavior. Firms should also collect data on diversity, employees' perceptions, and training effectiveness; introduce behavioral "nudges"; and rethink policies.

organizations, worried about a backlash, make UB training voluntary. As a result it's embraced only by people who are already familiar with bias and interested in reducing it. Second, 91% of the respondents indicated that their firms don't collect information on the metrics they claim to care about, such as the race and gender of new hires and recipients of promotions and employee recognition awards. It's hard to improve something you're not even tracking. Third, 87% of the respondents indicated that at their firms UB training doesn't go much past explaining the science behind bias and the costs of discrimination in organizations. In fact, only 10% of training programs gave attendees strategies for reducing bias. Imagine a weight-loss program that told participants to step on the scale and left it at that. The idea that we can reduce our bias simply by being aware of it is the fatal flaw in most UB training. In fact, most programs end exactly where they should start.

A More Effective Model

Successful UB training gives people concrete tools for changing their behavior. It helps them better understand others' experiences and feel more motivated to be inclusive.

Consider an approach that Patricia Devine of the University of Wisconsin and her colleagues have developed, called "prejudice habit-breaking." Like conventional UB training, it teaches what implicit bias is, how it's measured, and how it harms women and people of color. After being educated, participants take the Implicit Association Test, which demonstrates that we all fall prey to unconscious bias to a degree, and then get feedback on their personal level of bias. Next they're taught how to overcome bias through a combination of strategies. These include calling out stereotyped views, gathering more individualized information about people, reflecting on counterstereotypical examples, adopting the perspectives of others, and increasing interactions with different kinds of people. After learning about each strategy, participants are asked to come up with examples of how they could use it in their own lives. They're taught that the strategies reinforce one another and that the more they're practiced, the more effective they will be.

This approach really works. In a longitudinal experiment, Devine and her colleagues had 292 college students participate in prejudice habit-breaking with a focus on race. Two weeks later the attendees noticed bias in others more than students who hadn't participated did, and were also more likely to label that bias as wrong. Two years later the researchers went back to a subset of the students and found that those who had participated were still more likely to speak out against bias than students who had not.

Using similar techniques, the same researchers trained STEM faculty at the University of Wisconsin to reduce gender bias. Afterward, departmental hiring patterns began to change. Over the next two years the proportion of female faculty hired in departments that had undergone the training rose from 32% to 47%; in departments that hadn't received the training, the hiring of women remained flat. Faculty members in participating departments—both women and men—reported feeling more comfortable bringing up family responsibilities and even that colleagues valued their research and scholarship more, an independent survey conducted months after the workshop found.

The companies we've seen get good results from UB training take an approach similar to Devine's. In addition, they have both individuals and the organization track and reflect on progress and identify where broader change is needed. We observed this at the pharmaceutical company, where we conducted a three-month study with about 400 people. Six weeks after UB training there, participants reported greater feelings of inclusion, showed less bias and prejudice, and made greater commitments to organizational change than the employees who hadn't participated. Moreover, after the company worked to eliminate bias from its performance reviews, employees felt that they seemed fairer, and data analyses confirmed that their perception was accurate.

Now let's examine in greater depth the elements of successful UB training and the complementary measures that should be taken to reinforce its goals.

1. Stress That "You Hold the Power"

UB training needs to help employees *act* on their awareness of bias. The idea is to empower them to change while cutting off their escape route—the inner voice that says, "I'm born like this, and there's nothing I can do about it." Here are some ways to do that.

Overcome denial

Even if we're aware of our bias, we're often ignorant of its extent and its consequences. A large-scale audit of human resource managers conducted by Devah Pager and Lincoln Quillian, for instance, found clear evidence of discrimination against Black candidates in hiring. Over seven months in 2001, matched pairs of 23-year-old college students were asked to apply to 350 entry-level job openings in Milwaukee that had been randomly selected from a newspaper's Sunday classified section and a state-sponsored online job site. The applicants were two white students (one with a fictional criminal record and one without) and two Black students with the same profiles as the white applicants. The difference in the responses the applicants got was striking: Thirty-four percent of white students without records and 17% of white students with records received callbacks. Only 14% of Black students *without* records got callbacks, and a mere 5% of Black students with records did. Yet in a follow-up survey the managers indicated that they had no racial preference. Denial is widespread, but if people don't admit bias exists, they can't address it.

One of the issues is that traditional UB training tends to focus on extreme cases of abuse and harassment, giving employees another easy out: "I'd never do that," they say and tune out. While it's important to cover the extremes, training should look mostly at scenarios where leaders and employees subtly exclude others or downplay their contributions—one of the most widespread and insidious forms of bias.

Microsoft's online UB training, which is also available publicly, includes videos depicting various everyday workplace scenarios. In one, the only woman on a team tries to add her views and is interrupted multiple times until another member finally notices and asks her to speak.

Highlighting common forms of bias is also helpful when addressing more-blatant discriminatory behavior. Starbucks took an approach similar to Microsoft's when designing a new antibias training in reaction to a highly publicized 2018 incident in one of its Philadelphia stores. One day in April, two African American entrepreneurs arrived at a Starbucks store for a meeting. They sat without ordering, waiting for a local businessman to join them. The store manager asked them to either place an order or leave, and then called 911 when they did not. The police arrived and arrested them. The chain's leadership responded by closing all 8,000 of its U.S. stores for half a day of UB training focused on race. During it, leaders gave concrete examples of how bias can show up in stores, such as when employees treat customers differently on the basis of their skin color or make assumptions about how they'll behave because of their appearance.

Focus on the potential for growth

According to the respondents in our recent survey of nearly 1,300 working adults in the United States, learning that the brain is malleable and capable of positive change is the single most effective component of antibias training. Participants need to be taught that while bias is normal, it's not acceptable or unavoidable.

To help its employees and managers grow, the Canadian energy company Suncor encourages them to write in a "reflection notebook" about any instance in which they saw themselves acting with bias. They're also asked to think about the life experiences that shaped their biases.

Microsoft's UB training prompts participants to think more deeply about the examples of bias depicted in its videos. For instance, one shows a team discussion of who is most suited to lead a project. After watching it, participants are asked to indicate which of various statements made during the discussion are valid: (1) Technical understanding is important when leading a technical project; (2) Cynthia's young children will make it harder for her to be fully committed to the project; (3) Ravi's introverted nature makes him an unsuitable project leader; and (4) Gerry's relaxed demeanor would not serve this project's goals. The participants learn that only the first statement is valid. There is no evidence that having children, being introverted, or having a relaxed demeanor negatively affects a project leader's effectiveness.

Provide examples of how to change behavior
Each section of Microsoft's training includes a best practice for overcoming bias, such as "examine your assumptions." Participants are told, "The next time you catch yourself making a judgment about someone's background or working preference, ask yourself, could this be an asset? This is a simple way of reframing your thinking about a person or a situation." The training also teaches employees that they can counteract bias when hiring or assigning projects by clearly identifying the requirements of a role before evaluating potential candidates.

At one public relations company, the chief diversity officer works with various divisions to examine practices like customer interactions and hiring, identify where unconscious biases are prevalent, and help employees address them. Working with human resources, she found that performance reviews were biased: Women received less helpful feedback than men did. Why? The forms included a self-assessment, which managers read before filling out the feedback forms. Women, consistent with research findings, were less likely to promote themselves and were harder on themselves than men were. By eliminating self-evaluations, HR was able to reduce bias against women in managers' feedback. Examples like this are used in the company's UB training to concretely show how bias can be effectively addressed through changes in behavior.

Break stereotypes

Stereotypes we hold about ourselves and others profoundly influence our behavior. For instance, one of us (Coffman) has found that lack of confidence in their own talent leads women in fields stereotypically considered "male," like technology, to behave in ways that can jeopardize their success, such as suggesting fewer ideas, particularly when working with men, and not applying for roles for which they are qualified. But encouraging trainees to present examples that defy stereotypes can reduce bias. In one experiment by Nilanjana Dasgupta and Anthony Greenwald, students exposed to images of admired African Americans showed a weaker preference for white individuals. In another study that Dasgupta and Shaki Asgari did, female college students were less likely to view leadership and math as male domains after encountering female faculty members in those departments at their school.

Exposure to counterstereotypical information reduces prejudice and results in more-positive interpersonal interactions. Leaders of Corning, the manufacturer of high-tech glass and ceramics products, provide it as part of a broader initiative to address unconscious bias. Intersections, a learning site on Coming's internal community platform, hosts *Collective Voices,* a podcast series that showcases employees and leaders across the business discussing diversity, equity, and inclusion and sharing personal experiences. In some episodes employees and leaders talk about times they behaved in a biased manner—for example, by stereotyping a colleague because of his or her affiliation with a certain political or racial group. Their vulnerability helps others examine their own biases. Some of the stories have opened up discussions of counterstereotypical examples, such as women who are thriving in traditionally male roles, showing that there are ways for everyone to succeed in the organization. Since the launch of the podcast, which has become quite popular, internal surveys have revealed that employees are more comfortable talking about their mistaken views and find themselves relying less on stereotypes.

2. Create Empathy

Research shows that we have less empathy for people who seem different from us and are likely to treat them worse as a result. That's why connecting with others through empathy can improve our interactions across racial, gender, and other differences. Let's look at some ways to nurture empathy.

Offer opportunities to take the perspective of others

We don't put ourselves in someone else's shoes naturally, much research finds, but doing so can lead to greater interest in others' welfare and more-positive relationships. In laboratory studies, instructing participants to take another person's point of view has been found to reduce bias against stigmatized groups, such as African Americans, and to suppress unconscious prejudices. In one study a group of white Americans watched clips from the movie *The Joy Luck Club* and were asked to put themselves in the place of the Chinese American heroine, June. In comparison with a control group, participants later showed less implicit prejudice toward "outgroups" (people who were not like them). During the UB training at Starbucks, attendees who were shown videos in which employees from minority groups told their stories were asked to adopt the perspective of those colleagues.

Hold small group discussions

These create opportunities for people to learn about others' views and experiences. About every seven weeks, as part of an ongoing training called the Third Place development series, Starbucks provides new guided UB learning and discussion modules, which are delivered on iPads in its stores for retail employees and on the company's intranet for the rest of the workforce. The topics are crowdsourced from leaders of different departments, including human resources, employee development, and inclusion and diversity. But employees also can suggest areas where they feel they could use more education and support. Employees are given time off to go through each module in groups of three to five people and discuss the questions it poses. Each session is 30 minutes for baristas and other nonmanagement employees, and 60 minutes for managers and above.

Discussions can also occur virtually. On Corning's Intersections site, employees talk about issues related to inclusion in an online forum, where a moderator is available to answer questions and provide resources.

3. Encourage Interactions Among People from Different Groups

These can be a powerful antidote to bias. Research shows that white people who've had few interracial encounters often experience anxiety when interacting with Black people and try to avoid them altogether. But forming relationships with members of other groups can widen our social networks, decrease our stress around people who are different from us, and reduce our prejudices. Here are some effective methods for building them.

Expand inner circles

Training sessions themselves can help people get to know colleagues who are unlike them, even when the sessions are virtual. In our survey of nearly 1,300 working adults, respondents said they benefited from the opportunities that training offered to interact with diverse colleagues and to examine whom they had contact with most often. The success of this kind of effort is obviously tied to how diverse a workforce is in the first place. The fact that it can cause discomfort should not be a barrier. Research has shown that moderate discomfort is a critical catalyst for the introspection that can lead to more-egalitarian behavior.

At Starbucks pulse surveys and interviews with employees revealed that the discussions about the UB modules, which were open to all employees, allowed colleagues with different experiences and backgrounds to learn about one another and create new connections and made workers more empathetic.

Nurture curiosity

The natural desire to acquire new knowledge and information can reduce prejudice and discriminatory behavior, research by Gino finds. (See "The Business Case for Curiosity," September–October 2018.) Curiosity prompts us to get to know our colleagues better rather than make assumptions. UB training can encourage it by having people work together in diverse teams. At its UB training the multinational professional services firm EY assigns colleagues from varying cultural backgrounds to teams and encourages them to ask one another questions, find out what bias means to each person, and explore how to overcome it together.

Starbucks organizes regular sessions featuring outside speakers, from successful Black entrepreneurs to well-regarded influencers who belong to other minority groups or have disabilities. The aim is to spark interest in people whose experiences employees may not be familiar with. Attendees are invited to practice asking curious questions.

Urge employees to track their interactions

UB training should encourage people to reflect on how they spend their time at work and with whom. When they're handing out assignments, do their choices indicate bias? Whom do they gravitate toward in brainstorming sessions and spontaneous conversations?

When Gino coached a group of leaders on unconscious bias, she asked them to review their calendars to see whom they had met with in the previous month and whom they invited to meetings, and to think back about whom they called on to speak during those meetings. The data was eye-opening: People of color were not invited to meetings as often as white individuals, were called on less frequently in meetings they did attend, and met informally with their bosses less often. And when managers at a financial services firm analyzed investment opportunities and deals they'd passed on to colleagues, they found evidence of gender bias: More men than women were offered those opportunities.

4. Encourage Good Practices and Continued Learning

If leaders want their organizations to become more equitable and diverse, they need to help employees implement the lessons of UB training. Here are some measures they can encourage people to take.

Commit to improvement
UB training should offer leaders and employees alike time to thoughtfully consider their motivations for reducing bias. Some may want to gain a reputation for always striving to be inclusive. Some might buy into an organizational goal such as better serving diverse customers by creating a diverse workforce. Or they may want to address UB simply because it's the right thing to do. No matter what the goal, choosing a specific reason for a commitment is a first step toward improvement.

Choosing to commit is easier when participants see evidence of how unconscious bias affects their work. For instance, a large company that Gino worked with showed racial bias in performance evaluations. After HR directors reviewed the data, they and the company's senior leaders committed to eliminating unfair practices.

Find a mentor and solicit feedback
We often lack a clear sense of our own bias and how it affects others. One male leader we coached learned from a trusted colleague that in meetings he frequently interrupted people—primarily women—and often attributed women's ideas to their male colleagues. Once his eyes had been opened, he began paying closer attention to how he managed meetings.

At UB training, participants might identify a mentor who could observe their behavior for bias or advise them on how to solicit feedback from others. Team members may feel more comfortable providing input anonymously or may appoint one person to monitor meetings for signs of bias. Accepting that we're biased isn't easy, but learning from feedback is key to becoming more inclusive.

Track improvement

It's crucial to hold people accountable by monitoring whether behaviors truly change over time. When the leaders at the pharmaceutical company tracked their practices, they saw differences in their promotion patterns during the two years after their UB training. Similarly, the managers at the financial services firm were more unbiased and fair in their assignment of deals after they started tracking whom they passed their deals on to.

5. Set a Broader Strategy for Broader Impact

When organizations make a broad commitment to fostering diversity, equity, and inclusion, employees' buy-in increases. In our survey of more than 500 employees, participants reported taking UB training more seriously when it was accompanied by resounding institutional support demonstrated through thoughtfulness, time, and money. Here's how organizations can provide such support.

Build the foundations

First, organizations can collect data on the representation and dispersion of people from different groups across the business, employees' perceptions of inclusion, and where diversity-related process failures might be occurring (such as during hiring or performance reviews). That data will suggest which training topics might have the greatest impact on employees. Leaders can also establish a committee to oversee and report on progress toward diversity, equity, and inclusion goals. These endeavors will need dependable funding. At Starbucks, which has made a multiyear financial commitment to reducing bias, Molly Hill, the company's vice president of learning, development, and partner experience, says it speaks volumes that her team doesn't need to ask for a training budget every year—the money is allocated to the initiative by default.

Measure the effectiveness of UB training

This is critical to improving the training over time. It involves, first, gathering data on engagement with the training itself. Microsoft does that with participant surveys and by studying what makes employees, teams, and units most likely to consume UB training content. Starbucks similarly assesses engagement with antibias materials through pulse surveys of employees.

Second, organizations must track the outcomes they're trying to change. To promote improvements, companies like Microsoft and Corning publish demographic employment data in public reports each year. Starbucks tracks customer engagement with employees in different stores, asking whether their efforts are improving customer experiences.

Asking employees directly affected by bias to share their experiences before and after companywide UB training can also help leaders understand whether meaningful change is occurring. One way to do this would be through surveys done just before and a few months after the training.

Nudge people to make better decisions

After training, organizations can establish what behavioral scientists call "nudges"—measures that prompt people to engage in new strategies. For example, before managers write performance reviews, they might be reminded to avoid giving feedback about employees' personalities. Recruiters might be asked to reflect on key job requirements before discussing candidates. In these ways organizations can ensure that training lessons influence employees' everyday behavior.

Review and rethink policies

The leaders of Starbucks revised store policies that they believed led employees in Philadelphia to call the police on the two Black men.

The company issued clear guidelines stating that everyone was welcome to spend time in its stores, with or without making a purchase. And employees facing a challenging situation were encouraged to move beyond their gut reaction by consulting a checklist, considering the context, and seeking advice from others before taking action. Store managers were taught to ask, "Would I take this action with any customer in the same circumstances?"

As Starbucks recognized, UB training alone can't stamp out bias. Systemic changes are needed as well. Leaders should revise long-standing practices that unfairly disadvantage certain groups, such as relying on unstructured interviews or self-assessments. When managers at the financial services firm realized there was a gender bias in the way they assigned deals, they instituted a regular review to ensure that it stopped happening.

Leaders' desire for their companies to be more diverse, equitable, and inclusive has never seemed stronger. But conventional UB training programs aren't delivering the changes they're supposed to produce. By following our blueprint, organizations can create programs that inspire people to more courageously examine and improve their behavior. By replacing superficial, one-shot training with longer-term efforts that do a better job of helping people understand their own unconscious biases and see how to overcome them and measure their progress, leaders can turn their workplaces into environments where everyone truly feels a sense of belonging and appreciation.

Originally published in September–October 2021. Reprint R2105H

Why You Aren't Getting More from Your Marketing AI

by Eva Ascarza, Michael Ross, and Bruce G. S. Hardie

WHEN A LARGE TELECOM COMPANY'S marketers set out to reduce customer churn, they decided to use artificial intelligence to determine which customers were most likely to defect. Armed with the AI's predictions, they bombarded the at-risk customers with promotions enticing them to stay. Yet many left despite the retention campaign. Why? The managers had made a fundamental error: They had asked the algorithm the wrong question. While the AI's predictions were good, they didn't address the real problem the managers were trying to solve.

That kind of scenario is all too common among companies using AI to inform business decisions. In a 2019 survey of 2,500 executives conducted by *Sloan Management Review* and the Boston Consulting Group, 90% of respondents said that their companies had invested in AI, but fewer than 40% of them had seen business gains from it in the previous three years.

In our academic, consulting, and nonexecutive director roles, we have studied and advised more than 50 companies, examining the main challenges they face as they seek to leverage AI in their marketing. This work has allowed us to identify and categorize the errors marketers most frequently make with AI and develop a framework for preventing them.

Let's look at the errors first.

Alignment: Failure to Ask the Right Question

The real concern of the managers at our telecom firm should not have been identifying potential defectors; it should have been figuring out how to use marketing dollars to reduce churn. Rather than asking the AI who was most likely to leave, they should have asked who could best be persuaded to stay—in other words, which customers considering jumping ship would be most likely to respond to a promotion. Just as politicians direct their efforts at swing voters, managers should target actions toward swing customers. By giving the AI the wrong objective, the telecom marketers squandered their money on swaths of customers who were going to defect anyway and *underinvested* in customers they should have doubled down on.

In a similar case, marketing managers at a gaming company wanted to encourage users to spend more money while they were playing its game. The marketers asked the data science team to figure out what new features would most increase users' engagement. The team used algorithms to tease out the relationship between possible features and the amount of time customers spent playing, ultimately predicting that offering prizes and making the public ranking of users' positions more prominent would keep people in the game longer. The company made adjustments accordingly, but new revenues didn't follow. Why not? Because managers, again, had asked the AI the wrong question: how to increase players' engagement rather than how to increase their in-game spending. Because most users didn't spend money inside the game, the strategy fell flat.

At both companies, marketing managers failed to think carefully about the business problem being addressed and the prediction needed to inform the best decision. AI would have been extremely valuable *if* it had predicted which telecom customers would be most persuadable and which game features would increase players' spending.

Asymmetry: Failure to Recognize the Difference Between the Value of Being Right and the Costs of Being Wrong

AI's predictions should be as accurate as possible, shouldn't they? Not necessarily. A bad forecast can be extremely expensive in some cases but less so in others; likewise, superprecise forecasts create more value in some situations than in others. Marketers—and, even more critically, the data science teams they rely on—often overlook this.

Consider the consumer goods company whose data scientists proudly announced that they'd increased the accuracy of a new sales-volume forecasting system, reducing the error rate from 25% to 17%. Unfortunately, in improving the system's overall accuracy, they increased its precision with low-margin products while reducing its accuracy with high-margin products. Because the cost of underestimating demand for the high-margin offerings substantially outweighed the value of correctly forecasting demand for the low-margin ones, profits fell when the company implemented the new, "more accurate" system.

It's important to recognize that AI's predictions can be wrong in different ways. In addition to over- or underestimating results, they can give false positives (for instance, identifying customers who actually stay as probable defectors) or false negatives (identifying customers who subsequently leave as unlikely defectors). The marketer's job is to analyze the relative cost of these types of errors, which can be very different. But this issue is often ignored by, or not even communicated to, the data science teams that build prediction models, who then assume all errors are equally important, leading to expensive mistakes.

Aggregation: Failure to Leverage Granular Predictions

Firms generate torrents of customer and operational data, which standard AI tools can use to make detailed, high-frequency predictions. But many marketers don't exploit that capability and keep operating according to their old decision-making models. Take the hotel chain whose managers meet weekly to adjust prices at the location level despite having AI that can update demand forecasts for different room types on an hourly basis. Their decision-making process remains a relic of an antiquated booking system.

Another major impediment is managers' failure to get the granularity and frequency of their decisions right. In addition to reviewing the pace of their decision-making, they should ask whether decisions based on aggregate-level predictions should draw on more finely tuned predictions. Consider a marketing team deciding how to allocate its ad dollars on keyword searches on Google and Amazon. The data science team's current AI can predict the lifetime value of customers acquired through those channels. However, the marketers might get a higher return on ad dollars by using more-granular predictions about customer lifetime value per keyword per channel.

Communication Breakdowns

In addition to constantly guarding against the types of errors we've described, marketing managers have to do a better job of communicating and collaborating with their data science teams—and being clear about the business problems they're seeking to solve. That isn't rocket science, but we often see marketing managers fall short on it.

Several things get in the way of productive collaboration. Some managers plunge into AI initiatives without fully understanding the technology's capabilities and limitations. They may have unrealistic expectations and so pursue projects AI can't deliver on, or they underestimate how much value AI *could* provide, so their projects lack ambition. Either situation can happen when senior managers are reluctant to reveal their lack of understanding of AI technologies.

Data science teams are also complicit in the communication breakdown. Often, data scientists gravitate toward projects with familiar prediction requirements, whether or not they are what marketing needs. Without guidance from marketers about how to provide value, data teams will often remain in their comfort zone. And while marketing managers may be reluctant to ask questions (and reveal their ignorance), data scientists often struggle to explain to nontechnical managers what they can and can't do.

We've developed a three-part framework that will help open lines of communication between the marketing and data science teams. The framework, which we've applied at several companies, lets teams combine their respective expertise and create a feedback loop between AI predictions and the business decisions they're meant to inform.

The Framework in Practice

To bring the framework to life, let's return to the telecom company.

1. What is the marketing problem we are trying to solve?

The answer to this question has to be meaningful and precise. For example, "How do we reduce churn?" is far too broad to be of any help to the developers of an AI system. "How can we best allocate our budget for retention promotions to reduce churn?" is better but still too vague. (Has the retention budget been set, or is that something we need to decide? What do we mean by "allocate"? Are we allocating across different retention campaigns?) Finally, we get to a clearer statement of the problem, such as: "Given a budget of $x million, which customers should we target with a retention campaign?" (Yes, this question could be refined even further, but you get the point.) Note that "How do we predict churn?" doesn't appear anywhere—churn prediction is not the marketing problem.

When defining the problem, managers should get down to what we call the *atomic* level—the most granular level at which it's possible to make a decision or undertake an intervention. In this case the decision is whether or not to send each customer a retention promotion.

As part of the discovery process, it's instructive to document exactly how decisions are made today. For example, the telecom company uses AI to rank customers (in descending order) by their risk of churning in the next month. It targets customers by starting at the top of that ranking and moves down it until the budget allocated to the retention campaign runs out. While this step seems merely descriptive and doesn't reveal how the problem might be reframed, we have seen many cases where it is the first time the data science team actually gets to understand how its predictions are used.

It's important at this stage for the marketing team to be open to iterating to get to a well-defined problem, one that captures the full impact of the decision on the P&L, recognizes any trade-offs, and spells out what a meaningful improvement might look like. In our experience, senior executives usually have a good sense of the problem at hand but have not always precisely defined it or clearly articulated to the rest of the team how AI will help solve it.

2. Is there any waste or missed opportunity in our current approach?

Marketers often recognize that their campaigns are disappointments, but they fail to dig deeper. At other times managers are unsure about whether the results can be improved. They need to step back and identify the waste and missed opportunities in the way a decision is currently made.

For instance, most airlines and hotels track measures of *spill* and *spoil: Spoil* measures empty seats or rooms (often the result of pricing too high); *spill* measures "lost trading days" on which flights or hotels filled too quickly (the result of pricing too low). Spill and spoil are beautiful measures of missed opportunity because they tell a very different story from aggregated measures of occupancy and average spend. To make the most of their AI investments, marketing leaders need to identify their spill and spoil equivalents—not in the aggregate but at the atomic level.

The first step is to reflect on what constitutes success and failure. At the telecom firm, the knee-jerk definition of success was "Did the targeted customers renew their contracts?" But that's too simplistic and inaccurate; such customers might have renewed without receiving any promotion, which would make the promotion a waste of retention dollars. Similarly, is it a success when a customer who was not targeted by a promotion does defect? Not necessarily. If that customer was going to leave anyway, not targeting her was indeed a success, because she wasn't persuadable. However, if the customer would have stayed if she'd received the promotion, an opportunity was missed. So what would constitute success at the atomic level? Targeting only customers with high churn risk who were persuadable and not targeting those who were not.

Once the sources of waste and missed opportunities are identified, the next step is to quantify them with the help of data. This can be easy or very hard. If the data team can quickly determine what was a success or failure at the atomic level by looking at the data, great! The team can then look at the distribution of success versus failure to quantify waste and missed opportunities.

There are cases, however, where it is difficult to identify failures at the atomic level. At the telecom firm, the data team wasn't examining which customers were persuadable, and that made it hard to classify failures. In such circumstances teams can quantify waste and missed opportunities using more-aggregated data, even if the results are less precise. One approach for the telecom firm would be to look at the cost of the promotion incentive relative to the incremental lifetime value of the customers who received it. Similarly, for the customers not contacted by the promotion, the team might look at the lost profit associated with the nonrenewal of their contracts.

Such tactics helped the telecom company identify customers who were being retained but at a cost greater than their incremental future value, high-value customers who had defected despite receiving retention promotions, and high-value customers who had not been targeted and left after the campaign. This quantification was possible because the data science team had a control group of customers—who had been left alone to set the baseline—to compare results against.

3. What is causing the waste and missed opportunities?

This question is usually the hardest, because it requires reexamining implicit assumptions about the firm's current approach. To find the answer the firm must explore its data and get its subject matter experts and data scientists to collaborate. The focus should be on solving the alignment, asymmetry, and aggregation problems we identified earlier.

Addressing alignment. The goal here is to map the connections between AI predictions, decisions, and business outcomes. That requires thinking about hypothetical scenarios. We recommend that teams answer the following questions:

In an ideal world, what knowledge would you have that would fully eliminate waste and missed opportunities? Is your current prediction a good proxy for that?

If the telecom team members had answered the first question, they would have realized that if their AI predicted perfectly who could be won over by the retention offer (rather than who was about to leave), they could eliminate both waste (because they wouldn't bother making offers to unpersuadable customers) and missed opportunities (because they'd reach every customer who was persuadable). While it is impossible to make perfect predictions in the real world, focusing on persuadability would still have led to great improvements.

After the ideal information is identified, the question becomes whether the data science team can make the required predictions with sufficient accuracy. It's crucial that the marketing and data science teams answer this together; marketers often don't know what can be done. Similarly, it is difficult for the data scientists to link their predictions to decisions if they don't have subject matter expertise.

Does the output of your AI fully align with the business objective?

Remember the gaming company that used AI to identify features that would increase user engagement? Imagine the gains if the company had created AI that predicted user profitability instead.

A common mistake here is falsely believing that a correlation between the prediction and the business objective is enough. This thinking is flawed because correlation is not causation, so you might predict changes in something that correlates with profitability but does not in fact improve it. And even when there is causation, it may not map 100% to the objective, so your effort may not fully achieve your final outcome, leading to missed opportunities.

At the telecom company, asking this third question might lead the team to think not only about persuadable users but also about the increase or decrease in their profitability. A persuadable user with low expected profitability should have a lower priority than a persuadable user with high expected profitability.

Addressing asymmetry. Once you have a clear map that links the AI prediction with the decision and the business outcome, you need to quantify the potential costs of errors in the system. That entails asking, How much are we deviating from the business results we want, given that the AI's output isn't completely accurate?

At the telecom company, the cost of sending a retention promotion to a nonpersuadable customer (waste) is lower than the cost of losing a high-value customer who could have been persuaded by the offer (missed opportunity). Therefore, the company will be more profitable if its AI system focuses on not missing persuadable customers, even if that increases the risk of falsely identifying some customers as being receptive to the retention offer.

The difference between waste and missed opportunity sometimes is difficult to quantify. Nevertheless, even an approximation of the asymmetric cost is worth calculating. Otherwise, decisions may be made based on AI predictions that are accurate on some measures but inaccurate on outcomes with a disproportionate impact on the business objective.

Addressing aggregation. Most marketing AI doesn't make new decisions; it addresses old ones such as segmentation, targeting, and budget allocation. What's new is that decisions are based on richer amounts of information that are collected and processed by the AI. The risk here is that humans are, by and large, reluctant to change. Many managers haven't yet adjusted to the frequency and level of detail at which the new technology can make old decisions. But why should they keep making those decisions at the same pace? With the exact same constraints? As we saw earlier, this sometimes results in failure.

The way to solve this problem is by conducting two analyses. In the first, the team should examine how it could eliminate waste and missed opportunities through other marketing actions that might result from the predictions generated. The intervention that the team at the telecom firm considered was a retention discount. What if the team incorporated other incentives in the decision? Could it predict who would be receptive to those incentives? Could it use AI to tell which incentive would work best with each type of customer?

The second type of analysis should quantify the potential gains of making AI predictions more frequently or more granular or both. At one retailer, for instance, the data science team had developed AI that could make daily predictions of responses to marketing actions at the individual-customer level, yet the chain's marketing team was making decisions on a weekly basis across 16 customer segments. While changing the way the decisions were made would obviously incur costs, would the retailer find that the benefits outweighed them?

Marketing needs AI. But AI needs marketing thinking to realize its full potential. This requires the marketing and data science teams to have a constant dialogue so that they can understand how to move from a theoretical solution to something that can be implemented.

The framework we've presented here has proven to be useful for getting the two groups to work together and boost the payoffs from AI investments. The approach we've described should create opportunities to better align AI predictions with desired enterprise outcomes, recognize the asymmetric costs of poor predictions, and change the decisions' scope by allowing the team to rethink the frequency and granularity of actions.

As marketers and data scientists use this framework, they must establish an environment that allows a transparent review of performance and regular iterations on approach—always recognizing that the objective is not perfection but ongoing improvement.

Originally published July–August 2021. Reprint S21042

Net Promoter 3.0

by Fred Reichheld, Darci Darnell, and Maureen Burns

ON A SCALE FROM 0 TO 10, how likely would you be to recommend our company to a friend?

As a consumer, you've probably encountered this sort of question dozens of times—after an online purchase, at the end of a customer service interaction, or even after a hospital stay. And if you work at one of the thousands of companies that ask this question of their customers, you're familiar with the Net Promoter System (NPS), which Reichheld invented and first wrote about in HBR almost 20 years ago. (See "The One Number You Need to Grow," December 2003.) Since then, NPS has spread rapidly around the world. It has become the predominant customer success framework—used today by two-thirds of the *Fortune* 1000. Why has it been embraced so enthusiastically? Because it solves a vital challenge that our financial systems fail to address. Financials can easily tell us when we have extracted $1 million from our customers' wallets, but they can't tell us when our work has improved customers' lives.

That's the objective of NPS. It gauges how consistently a firm turns customers into advocates, by tracking and analyzing three segments: *promoters,* customers who are so pleased with their experience that they recommend your brand to others; *passives,* customers who feel they got what they paid for but nothing more and who are not loyal assets with lasting value; and *detractors,* customers who are disappointed with their experience and harm the firm's growth and reputation. Promoters give a score of 9 or 10, passives a 7 or 8, and detractors a 6 or less. To calculate your firm's overall Net

Promoter Score, you subtract the percentage of your customers who are detractors from the percentage who are promoters.

While that arithmetic might seem simplistic, the full system is intended to inspire teams to deliver experiences that are not merely satisfactory but remarkable. When customers feel cared for, they come back for more and bring their friends.

The power of customer advocacy is evidenced by the remarkable success of NPS leaders. Consider the 11 public firms highlighted in Reichheld's most recent book, *The Ultimate Question 2.0*. Over the past decade their median total shareholder return was five times the U.S. median (for public companies with revenues of more than $500 million as of 2010). Those results motivated more firms to track their Net Promoter Scores—and some to report them to investors.

Unfortunately, self-reported scores and misinterpretations of the NPS framework have sown confusion and diminished its credibility. Inexperienced practitioners abused it by doing things like linking Net Promoter Scores to bonuses for frontline employees, which made them care more about their scores than about learning to better serve customers. Many firms amplify the problem by publicly reporting their scores to investors with no explanation of the process used to generate them and no safeguards to prevent pleading ("I'll lose my job if you don't rate me a 10"), bribery ("We'll give you free oil changes for a 10"), and manipulation ("We never send surveys to customers whose claim was denied"). No details are provided about which customers (and how many) were surveyed, their response rates, or whether the survey was triggered by a specific transaction. Reports rarely mention whether the research was performed by a reliable third-party expert using double-blind methodology. In other words, some firms have turned Net Promoter Scores into vanity statistics that damage the credibility of NPS.

Over time we realized that the only way to make the system work better was to develop a complementary metric that drew on accounting results, not on surveys. We needed one that would illuminate the quality (and the likely profitability) of a firm's growth. It had to be based on audited revenues from all customers, not just on a potentially biased sample of survey responses, so that it would be

Idea in Brief

The Problem

The widely popular Net Promoter System has been misused and misunderstood.

The Cause

Firms corrupted a valuable metric, the Net Promoter Score, by making it into a target and reporting unaudited vanity statistics that hurt the credibility and usefulness of NPS.

The Solution

An accounting-based counterpart for the Net Promoter Score, *earned growth rate*, provides firms with a clear, data-driven connection between customer success, repeat and expanded purchases, recommendations, a positive company culture, and business results.

far more resistant to gaming, coaching, pleading, and the response biases that plague the results of nonanonymized surveys. We're confident we've successfully developed that metric.

In this article we introduce *earned growth* as the accounting-based counterpart for the Net Promoter Score, one that will reinforce the effectiveness of NPS, providing firms with a clear, data-driven connection between customer success, repeat and expanded purchases, word-of-mouth recommendations, a positive company culture, and business results.

The Origin of Earned Growth

The superior economics of companies with high Net Promoter Scores prove that generating more promoters (assets) and fewer detractors (liabilities) drives sustainable growth. But we knew we needed to reinforce NPS in a more objective way. Even when augmented with digital signals and big-data tracking, survey scores are inherently soft. Executives (and investors) need a hard metric to which people can be held accountable.

Reichheld had his "aha!" about earned growth while studying an investor presentation slide in preparation for a keynote at First Republic Bank's executive conference. The bank had quantified how much of its growth resulted from customers' coming back for more—and bringing their friends. The slide showed that existing customers accounted for 50% of the growth in deposit balances, and referred customers another 32%. In other words 82% of the bank's growth in deposits came from delivering great customer experiences. In loans 88% of growth resulted from making current customers happy.

The bank has data on referrals because it asks each new customer about the primary reason for selecting the bank and records the answer in the customer's file. The bank's customer accounting system automatically consolidates households with any related small businesses, so the bank can also easily see how much existing customers' deposits and loan balances have grown. The primary reason First Republic collects this data is to prove to investors (and regulators) that its rapid growth is safe and high quality. The bank has been growing loans 15% a year in an industry that typically grows 2% to 3% a year. In many cases that would raise a red flag, since it might suggest the bank was lowering credit standards to gain share. But the data demonstrated that it was growing without adding risk. Its new business came from customers it already knew well—and from individuals referred by long-term customers.

The presentation slide inspired Reichheld to develop a new metric, *earned growth rate,* which measures the revenue growth generated by returning customers and their referrals. A related statistic, the *earned growth ratio,* is the ratio of earned growth to total growth. That is what First Republic illustrated in its slide—82% for deposits and 88% for loans. Since the bank's total loan growth was 15% a year, its earned growth rate in loans was 13.2%. We predict that few other banks will be able to match First Republic's earned growth performance, but we won't really know for sure until more banks start measuring and reporting their own earned growth statistics. We do know that the portion of new customers generated by referral at First Republic—71%—far exceeds the portion seen at its peers in retail banking (measured through Bain's NPS Prism research), where it ranges from 21% to 53%.

In a very different industry, Warby Parker, the direct-to-consumer pioneer in prescription eyeglasses, earns almost 90% of its new customers through referrals. Warby was one of the first places where we tested the earned growth framework. The metric helped us

FIGURE 6-1

Comparing the quality of two firms' growth

Companies with the same revenue growth may have starkly different earned growth rates. The hypothetical firms in this exhibit have increased revenue at a similar pace. But by looking closely at the sources of this revenue one can see that Company A has earned its growth by satisfying existing customers who come back for more and bring their friends, while Company B has generated significant revenue by aggressively buying new customers through advertising and promotions.

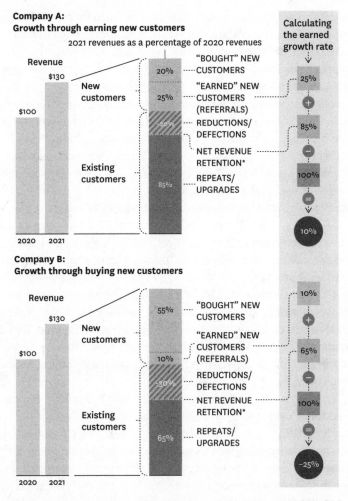

*To calculate net revenue retention, divide current period revenues from customers who were already on the books at the beginning of the period by total revenues from the previous period.

appreciate Warby's impressive loyalty-based growth. The company is a longtime practitioner of NPS and plans to continue using Net Promoter Scores as a key metric for internal management. But it also plans to augment its learning with earned growth.

Calculating Earned Growth

Although it's possible to estimate earned growth without access to internal company data, investors will demand accurate (and audited) statistics based on actual results. To gather the hard data needed, firms must upgrade their systems to incorporate customer-based accounting.

Basic customer accounting continually tracks costs and revenues for each customer over time, patterns of defection, reductions, and price discounts, along with segment identifiers including tenure. It also captures the reason each customer joined (for instance, whether the customer was "earned" through referral or reputation or "bought" through advertising, promotional deals, or commission sales), along with that customer's acquisition and onboarding costs.

Essentially, this is the core information required to estimate customer lifetime value (CLV). However, CLV is complex and incorporates probabilities and higher math (think actuarial science). Although it can generate powerful insights, its application is dependent on sophisticated expertise. CLV involves a projection about the value you can expect to gain from customers, while earned growth looks at real results and quantifies the value you actually received. Earned growth can help every team learn how it is performing—by keeping track of how much growth results from customers' coming back for more and bringing their friends.

Earned growth has two elements. The first is the back-for-more component captured by a battle-tested statistic called *net revenue retention* (NRR), which is used in several industries, most notably software-as-a-service (SaaS). Once you have organized revenues by customer, you can determine your NRR. Simply tally this year's revenues from customers who were with you last year, divide that amount by last year's total revenues, and express that figure as a percentage.

The second component is *earned new customers* (ENC). It is the percentage of spending from new customers you've earned through referrals (as opposed to bought through promotional channels). This component will take a bit more effort because firms must ascertain why new customers have come on board. We have developed a practical solution to this challenge, and while it may require some experimentation and refinement, ENC is important to track. The sooner you have a reasonable estimate of revenues from ENC, you can better focus your customer acquisition investments—and justify more investment in delighting current customers. Firms today undervalue referrals. They treat them as icing on the cake rather than an essential (perhaps *the most* essential) ingredient for sustainable growth.

To determine your earned growth rate, begin by calculating your NRR—since this is usually the larger of the two components. To get a sense of the importance of this statistic, consider the sensitivity of SaaS companies' valuations to modest shifts in their NRR. Firms with NRR over 130% are valued more than 2.5 times higher those with NRR below 110%.

Despite its importance, even experienced SaaS firms report NRR inconsistently. Some use samples of customers, some exclude new customers who also defect within the same period or customers with multiyear contracts, and so on. Our strong recommendation to regulators is to make this a formal GAAP metric with precise reporting rules.

Quantifying NRR may require homework in some industries. For example, not all brands consolidate household accounts across multiple product lines or services. Accounting for customers who join and defect within the same period must be handled consistently. Business-to-business firms will require rules for determining whether separate divisions (or purchasing units) of the same company represent one or multiple customers. But with today's sophisticated CRM technology, big-data tools, and a little analyst elbow grease, all that is doable, and it will require less work than arcane accounting metrics like goodwill and depreciation—which are demanded by GAAP but provide far less useful information.

Now let's consider how best to approach the second component of earned growth: the portion of revenues resulting from newly acquired earned customers. Few firms can quantify this today, so we have pioneered a solution that is proving effective in several ongoing beta tests. We add a relatively painless step to the process for onboarding new customers: asking them the primary reason they decided to give the company their business. By doing this right at the beginning of the relationship, we ensure that the decision is fresh in the customer's mind.

The reasons given are then sorted into earned versus bought categories. For example, if a customer chooses "trustworthy reputation" or "recommendation from friends or family," that customer and associated revenues count as earned. Customers who select "helpful salesperson," "advertisement," or "special deal or promotional pricing" are tagged as bought. Our goal is to develop a universally applicable process so that every firm can use the same methodology, resulting in comparable reported numbers. But for now a good solution is to pick the handful of reasons you expect customers will choose along with an open-ended "other" response where verbatim comments will help you adjust or augment the categories over time.

Tracking the behaviors of customers tagged as earned versus bought will help you determine their relative lifetime value, illuminating which customer segments and acquisition channels represent the best investments. In our consulting work we've seen that most firms find earned new customers to be far more profitable than bought customers, many of whom are revealed to be money losers over their life cycle. This customer-based accounting data is vital for implementing customer strategies such as those developed by our Bain colleague Rob Markey. (See "Are You Undervaluing Your Customers?" HBR, January–February 2020.) Viewing customers as a company's most important asset is just talk until each customer's value is tracked and quantified.

To determine your earned growth rate, add NRR and ENC together and then subtract 100%. Let's look at a hypothetical example. Company A's revenues grew from $100 in 2020 to $130 during 2021, or 30%. In 2021 customers who were on the books in 2020 accounted for $85 of revenues. Some of them expanded their purchases by a total of $5, but that growth was more than offset by other customers who reduced purchases by a total of $20, resulting in an NRR of 85%. New customers accounted for $45 in revenues—$25 from earned new customers (referrals) and $20 from bought new customers. Adding the NRR (85%) and ENC (25%) and then subtracting 100% results in a 10% earned growth rate.

Next, consider another hypothetical firm with the same reported revenue growth as Company A but very different sources of growth. Company B has an NRR of only 65%—far lower than Company A's. Although the two companies appear to be on the same trajectory, Company B is achieving its revenue growth by aggressively buy- ing new customers. (See the exhibit "Comparing the quality of two firms' growth.") That will almost certainly penalize current and future earnings and prove to be an unsustainable strategy. Today's GAAP accounting obscures this vital difference.

The real-world business impact of customer loyalty hasn't been lost on savvy investors and executives. By developing auditable sta- tistics, brands will be able to validate significant investments in pro- viding superior customer service. Now we'll look at two actual firms, FirstService and BILT, that have begun using the earned growth rate as a gauge of customer loyalty.

The Long-Term Economic Value of Referrals

When he was just a teenager, Jay Hennick founded FirstService as a pool-cleaning company. Fifty years later, FirstService generates more than $3 billion in annual revenues and employs 24,000 people. It is North America's largest manager of residential communities, such as condominiums and homeowners' associations, and it owns a port- folio of property services, including CertaPro Painters, California Closets, Century Fire Protection, and First Onsite.

FirstService began implementing NPS across all its businesses in 2008. When Reichheld met the current CEO, Scott Patterson, in 2011, Patterson explained that he was keenly interested in finding out more about how NPS could help his business leaders build even stronger relationships with customers. The more we learned about the company, the more intrigued we became (Reichheld eventually joined its board), mostly because it seemed to care about customer loyalty as much as we do. When Patterson heard about Reichheld's plans to develop earned growth, he responded: "That's a great idea. It perfectly reflects the way we think here at FirstService."

FirstService attributes much of its success to a customer-focused culture. All its local business leaders understand the enormous expense required to replace a customer lost through defection. They also know how much more efficient it is to earn new customers through word of mouth from existing customers. Patterson estimates that more than half of all new customers in its Residential business (that is, residential-community management) are referrals. In its California Closets unit, 70% of the quality leads are. In painting, CertaPro finds that 80% to 90% are. Local franchisees know that word-of-mouth leads are likely to result in good business (CertaPro closes on more than 90% of them—about twice the rate for other leads). And because franchisees remain close to the customer, they can learn who made a recommendation and ask the recommender what turned him or her into a promoter.

FirstService provides a compelling example of how investors win with customer loyalty. The firm listed its stock on the NASDAQ exchange early in 1995. When a Bain team examined all U.S. public companies that had revenues of at least $100 million that year—approximately 2,800 companies—and ranked them by their total shareholder return through the end of 2019, FirstService ranked eighth (ahead of superstars such as Apple), with an annual total shareholder return of almost 22% a year. One hundred thousand dollars invested in FirstService stock in 1995 would have grown to $13.6 million by 2019. By tracking and publishing auditable earned growth rates, companies like FirstService will be able to credibly demonstrate the sources of their advantage and thereby help investors understand the sustainability of growth generated by loyalty.

Patterson admits that he struggles to convince investors of the sustainable advantage that FirstService's customer-centric culture delivers. "They hear my words," he says, "but their financial mindset just can't make sense of them. They keep asking for the real secret sauce behind our impressive track record so they can assess our future." He views the development of a measurable science around earned growth as advantageous. He's not worried about giving away the secret sauce—after all, a service-based culture is hard to build and maintain.

BILT Pioneers Earned Growth Reporting

In 2016, BILT launched a mobile app to replace paper instructions with step-by-step 3D instructions for products requiring assembly, installation, setup, repair, or maintenance. Manufacturers and retailers send BILT computer-aided design files for products, and BILT converts them into digital animations with voice instructions and text prompts.

Amazon, IKEA, and Wayfair have acknowledged the negative impact that poor assembly processes have on customer experiences, and they've tested new methods to simplify home assembly. In 2017, IKEA purchased TaskRabbit, an online marketplace that today provides access to more than 100,000 freelancers, to make it easier for its customers to hire a handy person during the checkout process. Wayfair has partnered with Handy.com to offer a similar service. Earlier this year, Amazon began experimenting with a premium service that automatically includes assembly upon delivery.

BILT helps retailers eliminate the added expenses associated with assembly and customer support calls, and it gives buyers the knowledge and coaching needed to put items together on their own. BILT even keeps track of the time that people spend on each instruction screen, which helps manufacturers and retailers identify steps in the assembly process that are confusing or nonintuitive so that they can modify and improve the experience. The app also provides consumers with a virtual filing cabinet for all product registrations, warranty information, instructions, and troubleshooting tips. Updates to instructions saved in the filing cabinet are made in real time, so they never become obsolete. In other words, BILT helps retailers and brands improve customer experiences even after a product is assembled.

At the end of the assembly process, the BILT app generates a classic NPS survey asking how likely the consumer would be to recommend the product on a scale of 0 to 10, with an open-ended question about the reason for the rating and how the experience could be improved. Because of this, the app can provide retailers with rich customer feedback linked to specific SKUs and customer purchase records.

The firm's mission, according to its website, is to create "an experience so enabling and empowering, it transforms consumers into promoters of the brands we serve." It's fascinating to see the emergence of a business entirely devoted to helping other companies improve their NPS results.

When Reichheld first encountered BILT, in early 2020, its revenues were growing more than 175% a year. As happens at most startups, the business was eating up cash. But BILT's NRR was running at 150%, and most of its new customers came through referrals—resulting in an earned growth rate of 160%. That evidence persuaded Reichheld that the company's growth was sustainable. Since then, he has made a substantial investment in BILT and joined its board of directors.

Prosper by Helping Others

We had no idea how far-reaching our impact on the customer-centricity movement would be when Reichheld began writing about loyalty in *Harvard Business Review* more than three decades ago (in "Zero Defections: Quality Comes to Services," September–October 1990). We're proud of what we've helped companies accomplish, but we realize there is still very far to go. Early on, we saw that customer loyalty had little to do with marketing gimmicks and slick advertising, and we later proved that it generates bountiful economic advantages, including efficient customer acquisition.

Today we can establish that business success begins with leaders who embrace a fundamental proposition that their firm's primary purpose is to treat customers with loving care. That approach begets loyalty, which powers sustainable, profitable growth. It underpins the financial prosperity of great organizations and helps make them great places to work, but its effect has been notoriously difficult to quantify. It's time to get serious about measuring (and reporting) the progress made toward fulfilling that purpose and to recognize that improving the lives of the people we serve is the only way to win.

Originally published in November–December 2021. Reprint R2106E

How Chinese Retailers Are Reinventing the Customer Journey

by Mark J. Greeven, Katherine Xin, and George S. Yip

CHINA IS BOTH A LARGE and a fast-growing retail market—worth about $5 trillion in 2020—and highly digitized.

Given that the pandemic has made digital every retailer's strategic priority, it's not hard to see why the *Economist* opened 2021 with a cover story headlined "Why Retailers Everywhere Should Look to China."

In China online sales have grown about 25% in each of the past seven years and reached about $1.9 trillion in 2020, when they amounted to some 25% to 50% of total retail (compared with 10% to 20% in the United States). More than 90% of those sales are on mobile devices, compared with less than 50% in the United States. So it should be no surprise that Chinese companies and individuals have led the way in developing video retail, social commerce, community retail, retail-as-a-service, and many other new digital channels, including the super app, which provides an all-in-one experience for consumers by accessing various services and offerings.

Who are these leaders?

There's Douyin—known in the West as TikTok—which started as an entertainment app for sharing short videos and soon discovered that many users were commenting on popular videos by creating their own versions. Douyin encouraged participation by welcoming content creators, who often featured their favorite products and clothing styles, making the app a marketing tool. China's livestreaming market has reached $16.3 billion and is now integral to how people shop—which is why Walmart invested in Douyin.

Pinduoduo, the largest agriculture-focused platform in China, was founded in 2015 and is currently worth $175 billion. Sometimes described as "Groupon on steroids," it has gamified the shopping process, enabling groups to haggle with merchants, often via WeChat.

Then there's Li Jiaqi, a 28-year-old influencer who pioneered digital cosmetics retailing and is known as the Lipstick King. He boasts more than 7 million followers on Weibo and close to 40 million on Douyin. He once sold 15,000 lipsticks in just five minutes and tried on 380 lipsticks in a seven-hour livestreaming show. Li Jiaqi is the only male key opinion leader (KOL) for cosmetics and the best salesperson for beauty products in China. A former beauty adviser at L'Oréal, he has phenomenal influence: His recommendations can make or break a product launch. He demonstrates and recommends the products of multiple companies and is paid according to the sales he generates.

These innovators owe much of their success to the massive ecosystems of Alibaba, JD.com, Tencent, and, increasingly, Pinduoduo, ByteDance, and Meituan, which serve as key touchpoints for consumers. They attract Chinese retailers and international brands by leveraging ever more data in innovations such as Alibaba's Tmall Smart Selection (a product recommendation algorithm) and Meituan's highly sophisticated logistics routing algorithm. As Tencent's founder, Pony Ma, put it in an internal presentation in early 2020, "The era of smart retailing ignited by 'super connectivity' just kicked off." (That said, China's government is taking a harder line with its biggest online enterprises. In late 2020 it blocked the IPO of Ant Group, a fintech company spun out of Alibaba, at the last minute. Alibaba was also fined some $2.8 billion in April 2021 under the PRC's antitrust law.)

Retailers in Europe and the United States don't have access to such integrated ecosystems, but they can still usefully borrow from

Idea in Brief

The Challenge

Retailers in Europe and the United States are far behind China in digital retail.

Why It Exists

China's large and fast-growing market not only is highly digitized but also takes advantage of the massive ecosystems of Alibaba, Tencent, and others.

The Solution

To catch up, Western retailers can take five lessons from the Chinese experience: Create single entry points, embed digital evaluation in the customer journey, don't think of sales as isolated events, rethink the logistical fundamentals, and always stay close to the customer.

China's innovators. To identify how, we studied 25 Chinese digital retail companies, including the giants Alibaba, JD.com, Meituan, and Tencent; the emerging platforms ByteDance, Pinduoduo, and Ele.me; and successful brands such as Peacebird, Forest Cabin, Babytree, Soufeiya, and Xtep. In addition, our research benefited greatly from discussions with dozens of executives from Western companies, including Amazon, Apple, Daimler, Luxottica, Nestlé, Nike, PayPal, Philips, Siemens, Starbucks, and Walmart, along with Japan's Sogo & Seibu (department stores) and Russia's X5 Retail Group (a leading food retailer).

In this article we draw on that research to explain five lessons that Western companies can learn from China as they develop their own digital market offerings.

1. Create Single Entry Points

A single point online where customers can access all their potential purchases is the holy grail for retailers. China's digital giants have come close to achieving it by creating commerce ecosystems, general platforms offering portals for independent brands, and proactive automated product recommendations.

Ecosystems. For most digital retail consumers in China the first port of call is Taobao (Alibaba's mobile C2C portal) or Alipay, both of which give access to Alibaba's full ecosystem. Alipay, which is on almost every smartphone in China, integrates the platforms and service offerings of companies in Alibaba's huge retail network, enabling consumers to pay for any product or service they may find there, from Nike shoes to wealth management. Tencent's WeChat Pay provides similar benefits. Although users may not go online intending to make a transaction, WeChat Pay's deep integration with external platforms and specific brands means that they often end up doing just that. WeChat has pioneered a concept that allows any brand to develop dedicated but simple subapplications within the WeChat ecosystem. These typically fulfill functions such as e-commerce, coupons, and task management and are searchable on WeChat's home page. After the initial success of this innovation, most other super apps adopted it.

General platforms. In China's B2C e-commerce market, the world's largest, most independent retailers access customers through platforms provided by Tmall, which accounted for 64% of China's total B2C e-commerce market in 2020, and by JD.com (26%). But players such as VIP.com, Xiaohongshu (RED), and Ymatou are increasingly winning share with specialized platforms: Ymatou focuses on cross-border commerce in high-quality branded products, and RED, often dubbed a lifestyle sharing platform, targets Generation Z and combines social media and e-commerce. China's increasingly sophisticated digital consumers go to these sites for information and to access a community of like-minded customers.

Proactive product recommendations. Digital has shifted power relationships in retail. Recommendation algorithms, livestreaming by KOLs, and "native" (embedded online) e-commerce stores in TikTok have changed the traditional dynamic whereby a purchase begins with the customer's search for a product. For instance, Tmall Smart Selection uses an AI-powered algorithm backed by deep learning and natural language processing to recommend products to shoppers; it then communicates consumer interest to retailers so that they can increase inventory to keep up with demand. That kind of functionality reflects the growing power of retailers relative to manufacturers.

Chinese retailers go further than Amazon does in aggressively leveraging partners and third-party providers (including for logistics, which Amazon mostly manages itself), rather than building in-house capabilities. The result is that Chinese retailers are already profitably offering at scale most of Amazon's newer, not yet scaled-up offerings, such as health care, insurance, online groceries, smart home devices, and fashion.

Options for the West. The main challenge for established Western retailers is to get closer to where the consumer is online rather than direct digital traffic to where products can be purchased. To be sure, this is simpler in China because of its less-stringent data privacy rules. But Western companies could do more with the data available to them—for example, by using blockchain to guarantee privacy.

Companies in Europe, given their experience with the EU's tight General Data Protection Regulation, are well-placed to build an early advantage. The Otto Group, in Germany, is a case in point. A catalog retailer for decades, it initially struggled with the arrival in 2008 of Amazon and Zalando, a German online shoe and fashion company. But Otto made early moves into digital solutions, in particular leveraging ventures such as Risk Ident (fraud prevention) and Picalike (visual search) to build a platform with thousands of partners. Its online revenue for the fiscal year ending in February 2021 reached $17.8 billion.

Another example is Lydia, an emerging financial-services super app from France, which offers peer-to-peer payment, flexible sub-accounts, virtual cards for Apple Pay and Google Pay, and many other functions typically associated with Chinese super apps. To be sure, Europe and the United States have always had well-developed credit card services. But the real potential of super apps is not that they can replace credit cards or cash; it is that they provide a single entry point for consumers, incorporating financial services (lending, investment, insurance); e-commerce; goods delivery and tracking; ticketing for movies, live shows, airplanes, and trains; health care services (hospital reservations, medical consultations, pharmacies); taxi hailing; bike sharing; and a wide range of government functions, including taxation.

The same potential exists in Europe and the United States. Beyond privacy, we see few economic, political, or social barriers to one-stop solutions in the West. The cost to establish comprehensive platforms is relatively low, so new entrants will seize the opportunity if incumbents don't.

2. Embed Digital Evaluation in the Customer Journey

A key challenge for retailers is ensuring that consumers can efficiently and effectively evaluate their products in a transparent and unbiased way. With its strong emphasis on influencers and social media, Chinese retail evaluation is highly sophisticated and provides content much richer than what is available in the West.

Customer reviews. Simple scoring or comments on Tripadvisor and Amazon are no longer the standard for Chinese consumers, who provide thousands of detailed comments about products, brands, and shops on JD.com, Tmall, and Taobao, often with photos or videos attached.

Influencers. In the United States people follow key influencers such as Taylor Swift and Kylie Jenner primarily on Instagram, whereas China's opinion leaders have a presence on Weibo, WeChat, TikTok, and other platforms. A common criticism directed at Chinese influencers is that many of them are sponsored—but their neutrality isn't highly valued in Chinese culture. The relationship of an influencer and a consumer is that of a celebrity and a fan, and consumers often consult several influencers before making a decision.

Video livestreaming. Chinese consumers also frequently consult livestreamers, who consist of three main types: CEOs such as Dong Mingzhu of the appliance manufacturer Gree Electric and Li Bin of the electric car company NIO; movie actors and musical artists such as Li Xiaolu and Liu Tao; and professional sellers such as Li Jiaqi, who sold products worth $145 million on Singles' Day in 2019, and Viya, known as the number one "sister" of Taobao Live.

Independent platforms. In reaching a purchasing decision, Chinese consumers rely far more on independent knowledge platforms such as Zhihu and Zhishi Xingqiu (which are similar to Wikipedia and Quora) than do Western consumers, who might consult *Consumer Reports* for high-value products.

Options for the West. As Chinese consumers have become more-sophisticated users of tech products, they've started consulting multiple data sources. Western companies need to establish a presence on all the channels where consumers evaluate products—particularly video-based social media. That way they can overcome mistrust of promotional messaging and positive reviews on company sites. Currently the most popular livestreaming in the West runs on gaming platforms such as Twitch, whose tie-in with Amazon makes it a platform for influencer sales. Meanwhile, NTWRK, a mobile-first video shopping platform, features limited-edition products of brands such as Adidas, Guess, and Vans. On its platform the video game company Rooster Teeth and other popular influencers drive sales through product collaborations. Other Western retailers might consider this approach.

3. Don't Think of Sales as Isolated Events

Providing a seamless experience when and where the consumer chooses can radically increase the chances of purchase. In the digital realm China has achieved this in three ways.

Deeply integrated online and offline sales channels. At Alibaba's Hema Fresh supermarket, for example, consumers can make purchases while sitting at home, on the way to the market, or in the store. They might have fresh food delivered or decide to pick it up while shopping for other products. After JD.com invested in the supermarket chain Yonghui, in 2015, it connected Yonghui's offline supermarkets to the JD Daojia ("JD to Home") application, which was launched that year in collaboration with Dada, a local on-demand delivery company. (The two merged the following year.) This level of integration brings big advantages. For instance, when the billion-dollar fashion retailer Peacebird closed down its brick-and-mortar stores during the pandemic, it could quickly pivot to online selling, because its sales system no longer differentiated between online and offline.

Continuous purchasing opportunities. In China a purchase can be made at almost any point in an individual's entire online experience. A consumer might buy directly from an official WeChat account while chatting with friends or in one of WeChat's "mini program malls" or Alipay's mini program for a brand that has advertised in a friend's circle or been recommended in an alumni group. Entertainment and shopping are fully integrated as well. A Chinese consumer watching a TikTok video can click on clothes she likes and end up in a native store. Or she might follow a friend's recommendation on WeChat to buy a product at a discount via Pinduoduo.

AI-enabled interfaces. AI-powered chatbots such as Dianxiaomi, which can understand more than 90% of customers' queries, are widely used in China; they did most of the talking during its "Singles' Day" on November 11, 2020, when Alibaba's online transactions exceeded $74 billion. After-sales service, in terms of delivery, returns, and warranty, was conducted primarily online. According to recent statistics, 94% of online service at Alibaba is AI-enabled, and it earns customer satisfaction ratings 3% higher than service delivered by staffers.

Options for the West. Legacy businesses that are embracing digital approaches need to cut across the silos of online and offline selling that have been traditional in the West. Even General Motors, the granddaddy of offline manufacturing, now has more than 100 social media channels. Walmart, the archetypal brick-and-mortar retailer, announced in February 2020 that it would combine its store and online buying teams in one omnichannel merchandising group. As Zeina Belouizdad, Google's omnichannel product lead for Europe, the Middle East, and Africa, said in late 2018, "We are living in an omnichannel world. Nothing is linear anymore." Consumers don't distinguish between offline and online, and it is only for legacy reasons that the distinction still exists. Executives outside China should therefore consider aligning and centralizing their sales systems as part of digital transformation efforts.

The United States and large parts of Europe have digital platforms and promising new ventures that could facilitate such integration. Global retailers could potentially enhance their existing digital solutions by partnering with those businesses. For example, in the Netherlands, one of the largest European e-commerce markets, Jumbo supermarkets and the seafood retailer Schmidt Zeevis are taking advantage of the online supermarket Picnic. Consumers can choose where to buy their products and when, with smooth home delivery or in-store pickup options.

Although France's super app Lydia and other new ventures are promising, companies need to do much more to broaden purchase options. In China, QR code payment and facial recognition scans are now common on Alipay, WeChat Pay, and many other payment apps. In Europe, however, most retailers use contactless card payment or require payments to go directly through a bank app.

4. Rethink the Logistical Fundamentals

China combines old-fashioned methods and high-tech software to deliver faster and at lower cost than almost any Western retailer can. A same-city order with a retail chain takes less than half a day to arrive in a large urban center like Shanghai, while local supermarkets can usually deliver orders in under 60 minutes. This speed is due primarily to large-scale, born-digital logistics integrators like Cainiao. A smart network, Cainiao leverages independently owned hardware and infrastructure such as warehouses and delivery vans and optimizes them across the country. These operations have several key features.

Gig workers. Last mile or local delivery to a customer's door, which is usually expensive, is a major challenge. In China this link in the supply chain is supplied by migrant workers (from the provinces) on bicycles or electric scooters. They are typically employed on a piecework basis by third-party logistics companies such as Meituan, which serves small grocers and restaurants, or by large online-offline chains such as Hema Fresh. These workers constitute a large and cheap labor pool that few other countries can match.

Sophisticated routing technology. They may be riding bikes, but the workers are guided by routing software that speedily provides a large quantity of information. Once an order is placed, a middleware system subtracts it from the inventory, puts the information into the company's CRM system, chooses the nearest outlet for fast delivery, and alerts the nearest delivery worker. The delivery worker's app will even specify which stairs to take inside a building to get to the right floor, as instructions are passed on by the customer. As a result, delivery in China is extremely fast. Such efficiency enables workers to earn a good living, while employers can track each employee's contribution.

Free to the customer. The scale effects and highly efficient logistical operations keep delivery costs so low that most merchants can afford to cover them completely. (Fresh-food delivery is an exception: It costs six times as much as regular delivery in China.) If a purchase exceeds a certain amount (typically $15), or if a customer has brand membership through a loyalty program or for a token enrollment price, he or she can enjoy free delivery with speed.

Options for the West. Again, Western companies do not have access to an equivalent workforce, and navigating urban layouts can be challenging (imagine bike deliveries in Los Angeles). What's more, stricter labor regulation may make it harder to rely on gig workers. (That can be overcome, as evidenced by California's passage in November 2020 of Proposition 22, which preserved the nonemployee status of ride-share drivers.)

Companies will have to compensate by leaning more into tech. Many could digitize the back-end supply chain by deploying cloud-based warehouse management systems that are integrated across stores, enabling faster and more-flexible delivery services. Big data analytics will also contribute—subject to privacy constraints. In time, technology may even make it possible to take labor out of the equation, as autonomous vehicles and drones become feasible for physical delivery. For example, Ericsson, Einride, and Telia have partnered to launch 5G-powered driverless and environmentally friendly trucks. Nuro, a self-driving delivery startup, is teaming up with Domino's, Walmart, and CVS. And in the field of logistics competitors are working together to build huge data pools that will enable faster, better predictive analytics—as seen in the partnership of the rival vehicle telematics companies Geotab and Webfleet Solutions.

5. Always Stay Close to the Customer

In China customer loyalty in digital retailing is generated in large part by extraordinarily high levels of after-sales engagement by companies and loyalty programs that are integrated into both e-commerce channels and social media. Companies also work with influencers and cultivate fan communities of their own.

Radical engagement. Chinese retailers truly treat the customer as royalty. Most online shops allow free returns with no explanation within seven days of a purchase (excluding fresh produce). Customers may choose a convenient pickup time for their returned products. Retailers offer instantaneous personal assistance via chatbots. Free hotline support is readily available, often 24/7. For products that require on-site services (such as installation), customers may choose days and precise time slots. These services are often supplied by local shops that carry the brand. For example, the wooden-door producer Tata Pravesh treats its traditional distributors as after-sale service providers for customers purchasing from the online store. The distributors get the same financial return they would if the products had been sold in their offline shops.

Integration across entry points. Customers have as many touch-points with loyalty programs as they do with brands. Coupons and digital red envelopes (traditionally exchanged by relatives and friends during celebrations) are daily offerings on large platforms such as Taobao, Tmall, JD.com, and Meituan (for restaurant food order and delivery). Online shops offer deep discounts every day during certain hours to attract return customers and discounts for customers who make successful recommendations to friends on social media. Loyalty programs are integrated across all digital channels.

Influencer relationships. As noted, the Chinese rely heavily on key opinion leaders' recommendations; in many cases KOLs command more loyalty than the brands they recommend. Chinese retailers piggyback on that relationship by cooperating with these KOLs, who often become associated with a particular brand. Some KOLs cut across product categories, representing brands for each. For example, Viya sells everything from makeup and shoes to rice and even houses. She sold goods worth $4.5 billion in 2020 with a team of just 500 people.

Fan marketing. The home electronics company Xiaomi has created a huge base of loyal users who help promote the brand. Its fans will buy anything Xiaomi sells. Now the company has its own online ecosystem, having partnered with more than 300 producers to sell their products to its fans under the Xiaomi brand. On April 1, 2021, Xiaomi announced that it would invest $10 billion over the next 10 years to produce smart electric cars. The company has sharpened its industrial and project design capabilities to give products under its brand name a similar look and feel at an affordable price. This type of fan economy is steadily growing in China.

Options for the West. Western companies should leverage digital platforms to offer loyalty rewards more often, more explicitly, and in more places. They can also use their various channel partners to improve delivery and service. And continuous tech-enabled tracking of service delivery processes and customer engagement will motivate sales agents and other employees to attend to customers' needs.

In other aspects of customer engagement, Western retailers are not so far behind. The U.S. exercise equipment company Peloton's creation of an online community of users has been a major driver of its success and a source of innovative ideas. And at least one fast-fashion retailer, Shein, based in the United States but founded in China in 2008, uses influencers as its main channel to customers. It is hugely successful with this approach, generating multibillion-dollar revenues and challenging even Zara, the longtime leader in the sector.

———————

Western retailers lag their Chinese counterparts in leveraging customer data to make better business decisions, increase operational efficiency, and reduce costs. They need to integrate that data with offline businesses so that customers are visible, identifiable, and traceable both online and offline. Retailers need to establish contact with customers online through multiple touchpoints, including social media ecosystems, to increase their stickiness, loyalty, and activity. Digital retailing is an organizational transformation in the making. A famous Chinese saying has it that "a journey of a thousand miles begins with a single step." The new customer journey begins with many steps.

Originally published in September–October 2021. Reprint R2105E

The Circular Business Model

by Atalay Atasu, Céline Dumas, and Luk N. Van Wassenhove

IT'S EASY TO SEE WHY more and more manufacturing companies are talking about what's often called the circular economy—in which businesses create supply chains that recover or recycle the resources used to create their products. Shrinking their environmental footprint, trimming operational waste, and using expensive resources more efficiently are certainly appealing to CEOs.

But creating a circular business model is challenging, and taking the wrong approach can be expensive. Consider the case of Interface, an Atlanta-based commercial flooring company. In the 1990s its founder and CEO, Ray Anderson, declared that he wanted Interface to become "the first sustainable corporation in the world." To achieve that, the company would shift its business model from selling to leasing. It launched the Evergreen Services Agreement (ESA) program, with installation, maintenance, and removal of its flooring bundled under one monthly fee, making it possible for the company to keep used flooring materials out of landfills and recycle the valuable raw materials in them.

This unprecedented move was intended to close the loop of the commercial-carpeting supply chain, and Interface pushed hard to make it work, even going so far as to develop a network of carpet distributors to service clients across the United States on behalf of the company. But after seven years of strenuous sales efforts, Interface had acquired just a handful of lessees. The overwhelming majority of customers preferred to buy rather than lease their carpets, because carpet maintenance fell under the general heading of janitorial services, rendering its costs invisible to them. They could not easily see the upside to paying fairly high monthly fees. The ESA program was simply not scalable.

Happily, that wasn't the end of the story. In 2000 Interface shifted its focus from long-term leases to producing modular carpet tiles using sustainable materials, such as recyclable nylon fibers and recyclable vinyl backings. And as it turned out, manufacturing the new carpet tiles emitted 75% less carbon than the industry average. Combined with a transition to renewable energy on production sites, these innovations have shrunk Interface's total carbon footprint by 69%, according to company reports. Unlike leasing, the focus on recycling has leveraged what Interface does best: manufacturing and selling carpets.

Interface's experience shows that creating a sustainable circular business model depends on many factors, but perhaps the most important is choosing a pathway that aligns with a company's capabilities and resources—and one that addresses the constraints on its operations. In the following pages we identify the three basic strategies for circularity and offer a tool to help manufacturers identify which is most likely to be economically sustainable for them. Our recommendations draw on decades of research and consulting with dozens of manufacturers across the world.

Three Strategies for Circularity

Manufacturing companies—from the producers of products that serve the new economy to the more traditional companies that provide our clothing and furnishings—can create a circular business model in many ways. Most involve a combination of three basic strategies.

Retain product ownership (RPO)

In the classic version of this approach, the producer rents or leases its product to the customer rather than selling it. Thus the producer

Idea in Brief

The Problem

Manufacturing companies attracted by the promise of circular business models—in which used products can be recovered and reused or recycled—may struggle to make them sustainable.

Why It Happens

Managers all too often select circularity strategies that don't align with their resources, capabilities, and constraints.

The Solution

The three basic strategies for creating a circular business model are retaining product ownership, product life extension, and design for recycling. In determining what combination of these to adopt, managers should consider the ease of gaining access to used products and the ease of recycling materials, components, or the complete product. These factors, together with how much value is locked up in the product, determine how much value can be recovered from a given pathway to circularity.

---

is responsible for products when consumers have finished with them.

RPO is an interesting strategy for companies that offer complex products with a lot of embedded value. A good example is Xerox, which has for a long time leased its printers and photocopiers to corporate customers. This strategy may require companies to invest heavily in after-sales and maintenance capabilities, which may be more expensive for them and, ultimately, their customers than a strategy of sell and replace.

RPO can also work with simpler products when they are relatively expensive and seldom needed. For instance, promgoers have been renting tuxedos for decades, and the rental model is becoming more prevalent in an increasingly status-conscious society. The online fashion subscription service Rent the Runway, for example, rents designer clothes to people in need of a smart outfit for a one-off event. Its clothes may have little intrinsic value—in terms of their raw materials, for example—but their brand value can be significant.

Product life extension (PLE)

Companies applying this strategy focus on designing products to last longer, which may open up possibilities for markets in used products. Because a longer product life span means fewer purchases over time, this may seem like a bad idea for original-equipment manufacturers. But durability is a key competitive differentiator and provides a strong rationale for premium pricing, as we've seen with the outdoor-clothing manufacturer Patagonia and the luxury home-appliance company Miele. PLE can also help companies prevent their customers from defecting to a rival brand. Bosch Power Tools, for example, extends the life of its used tools by remanufacturing them, thereby enabling it to compete with new products from low-cost, low-quality producers.

Design for recycling (DFR)

Companies applying this strategy redesign their products and manufacturing processes to maximize recoverability of the materials involved for use in new products. This strategy often involves partnering with companies that have specific technological expertise or that may be best able to use the materials recovered. Adidas's six-year partnership with Parley for the Oceans is an example. Parley uses plastic waste to make textile thread from which Adidas manufactures its shoes and apparel. Their partnership reduces the amount of plastic waste in the world's oceans.

Determining which combination of the three basic strategies will unlock the most value for your company involves some practical and very specific questions, such as whether you can reclaim your product from the customer, whether it can be moved, and whether you can remanufacture it. Let's look now at how best to structure that discussion.

The Circularity Matrix

A circular business model is sustainable only if value can be economically recovered from the product. It might be realized through reusing the product, thereby extending the value of the materials and energy put into the manufacturing process, or by breaking it down into components or raw materials to be recycled for some other use. Value needn't be tangible, of course; as demonstrated by designer clothing, it is possible to create a circular business model in which value is almost entirely intangible.

In general, the greater the value locked into a product—whether in terms of its brand cachet, the resources consumed in manufacturing it, or the premium customers might pay for an environmentally friendly product—the greater the potential for creating a circular business model around it. External factors, such as regulations, secondary markets in used products, or active markets in commodity components, will also determine how much value manufacturers can extract from a circular model.

It is, however, difficult to know just how much of that value a circular business model could unlock. The Slovenian white-goods company Gorenje attempted to lease its washing machines, which would seem to be a plausible strategy for the product. Washing machines can last a long time, and their useful lives can be extended with careful maintenance. But consumers were sensitive to the fact that they would pay more over the life of the lease than they would to own the machines, while the services they expected from a leasing contract cost more than Gorenje was willing to spend on maintenance.

Assessing the feasibility of a given circularity strategy requires a careful calculation of value and costs and a certain amount of experimentation and piloting. However, companies can clarify their thinking by answering just two questions:

1. How easy is it to get my product back?

In Norway more than 97% of plastic bottles are recycled. That's because Norwegians are unusually enthusiastic about recycling—and also because a large retail network (including reverse vending machines) exists for bottle collection, supported by a government-run deposit-refund scheme. In other words, Norway has two key elements for making reverse supply chains work: public participation and infrastructure. Without them, access to used products for circularity can be challenging, as indicated by much lower rates of plastic-bottle collection and recycling in other parts of the world.

Another element to consider is the existence of secondary markets in used products and commodity markets into which extracted raw materials can be sold. Consumers will naturally be reluctant to relinquish used products with a high resale or exchange value (such as power tools and construction equipment), making it difficult for original sellers to close the circle. In those cases accessing used products might involve expensive buyback or trade-in programs, which is precisely why companies often consider a leasing business model: It is easier to recover products if you own them.

2. How easy is it to recover value from my product?

Extremely heavy or bulky products and those containing potentially hazardous materials may be easy for producers to reclaim legally but difficult and expensive to move and recondition. In a reverse supply chain, moving a washing machine, for example, will clearly be much harder and more expensive than moving an ink cartridge. It is also difficult to recover value when products are intricately constructed. Advanced smartphones and laptops, for instance, are less easily reconstituted than coarser-grained, modular devices such as desktop computers. Finally, the feasibility of value recovery will depend on the availability of cost-effective solutions for reformulating products. If time-intensive manual labor is required, used products must have enough value left in them to justify the investment.

The answers to those two questions help identify where a company belongs in a two-by-two matrix that presents the strategic options for creating a circular business model. (See "The circularity matrix.") Let's look now at each quadrant.

Hard to access and hard to process

Products in the top right quadrant may experience a level of wear and tear that precludes easy repair and remanufacturing, taking product life extension off the table, especially for products with relatively little value locked up in them. Those that are in good condition and still usable may also have a high resale value in customer-to-customer secondary markets, making it harder for the manufacturer

FIGURE 8-1

The circularity matrix

For companies looking to create circular business models for their products, the right model will involve one or more of three basic strategies: retain product ownership (RPO), product life extension (PLE), and design for recycling (DFR). The right strategy can be determined by how easily the manufacturer can get the product back and how easily value can be recovered from it. The challenges each company faces along each dimension will depend on its capabilities and competitive context and may change in response to innovations it and its competitors make.

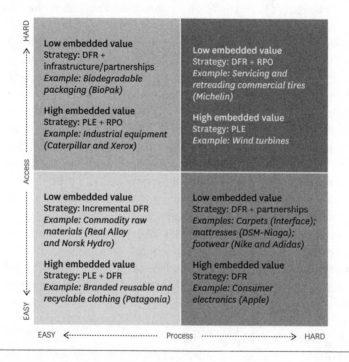

to access them for reconditioning. To prevent the loss of the value embedded in them, we advise manufacturers to consider a combination of design for recycling and retain product ownership.

The French tire manufacturer Michelin seems to be heading down that pathway, although it has not explicitly linked the two strategies. Along with committing to use 80% sustainable materials in its manufacturing, the company has acquired Lehigh Technologies, a Georgia-based maker of environmentally friendly rubber powders produced from ground-down end-of-life tires. Meanwhile, it is pivoting to RPO in many B2B markets, promising commercial fleets performance enhancements and cost savings for leasing tires. To deliver those benefits, Michelin's leasing businesses rely on modern information technologies. Its Effifuel division, for example, installs digital sensors in vehicles to monitor carbon emissions, fuel efficiency, and other performance metrics.

For companies in this quadrant, going circular may have low value potential even with expensive products containing lots of valuable ingredients. Wind turbines provide an extreme example: Although a lot of value was expended in creating them, their remote locations and size make them very difficult to access, while their composition and complex architecture make it hard to extract reusable materials or components. That's why we see wind turbines piling up in desert landfills.

That doesn't mean turbine companies should give up on circularity, but they should begin by considering how they can unlock value from the product through a strategy of product life extension. By investing in durability and modularity so that products will last longer and can be more easily maintained, companies could potentially open the door to an RPO model, whereby turbine manufacturers, rather than power companies, would retain ownership of and responsibility for the turbines. In the longer term they might be able to adopt a DFR strategy, making the turbines less reliant on nonrecyclable materials and easier to dismantle.

Easy to access but hard to process

The bottom right quadrant includes relatively low-embedded-value products such as carpets, mattresses, and athletic footwear. On the one hand, ease of portability and the absence of a lucrative secondary market create a strong likelihood that these products can be recouped from the consumer. On the other hand, they can't be easily reconditioned, and extracting materials from them is complex.

In such cases, going circular will involve product design for recycling. DSM-Niaga, a Dutch startup founded in 2014, developed a fully recyclable mattress consisting of six modular components, and carpets made from pure polyester rather than the industry-standard materials, which contain an indissoluble complex of chemicals including many known carcinogens. The mattress is easy to disassemble, allowing for easier maintenance (for example, the mattress covers are removable and washable), and the raw materials can be recycled at the end of the mattress's life. The homogenous design of carpets significantly facilitates material recovery and reduces the water and energy needed in the production process. The new carpets are also lighter, making transport and handling easier.

When products have relatively low value, companies—even very big ones—may need to find partners to make circularity work. Adidas, as noted earlier, provides one example. Its archrival Nike also works with partners: Nike Grind takes used athletic shoes and recycles them into materials for entirely new products, such as AstroTurf's playing fields and Future Foam's carpet padding. We see similar initiatives in other industries, from consumer goods to electronics.

Products in this quadrant include many small high-tech devices, such as smartphones, which have a lot of highly integrated components, toxic materials that are difficult to extract, and very short life cycles. These products typically have busy secondary markets, which is positive from an overall environmental perspective but impedes original manufacturers' access to them.

That is less a problem for the main manufacturers of high-tech consumer electronics. They often become the anchors in an industry ecosystem that creates exit barriers for device owners, thus lowering access barriers for the manufacturers. Apple is perhaps the definitive example. Customers buy, repair, and trade in their devices at Apple's own retail outlets, and their activity on those devices generates data that Apple owns. Of course, iPhones and iPads have an active secondary market, which normally would limit the company's recovery of them—but the speedy rollout of next-generation products and trade-in rebates incentivize consumers to relinquish their old Apple devices in exchange for discounted upgrades.

The easy access afforded by the dynamics of their ecosystems enables large-device manufacturers to invest heavily in DFR as their pathway to circularity. In 2018 Apple introduced Daisy, a robot capable of disassembling up to 200 iPhones an hour to recover valuable materials such as cobalt, tin, and aluminum for use in brand-new phone components.

Hard to access but easy to process

The top left quadrant includes products whose use makes them difficult to retrieve. Takeout food packaging, for example, may contain easily recyclable materials but very often winds up in landfills because of the food residue on it, which is costly to remove. Here the strategy should be DFR, with a focus on the recovery infrastructure. The solution devised by the Australian food-packaging company BioPak was to introduce not only fully compostable packaging but also a composting service extending to more than 2,000 postal codes across Australia and New Zealand, in partnership with local waste-management businesses. Customers can toss compostable packaging together with food scraps directly into an organic-waste bin for collection. BioPak claims that 660 tons of waste have been diverted from landfills as a result of the service.

As embedded value increases, secondary markets tend to appear; these can make access to products more difficult for the original manufacturer. RPO gets around the access problem, but it often proves challenging, even for companies whose products may seem well suited to an RPO strategy. One washing-machine producer we worked with abandoned its plans to offer a leasing option because of the expense of retrieving and transporting used machines to a company facility for remanufacture and reconditioning. Companies in a similar position often use traditional purchase plus a comprehensive service guarantee to extend product life.

The greater the embedded value, the more common are PLE and RPO combinations, because RPO both facilitates access to parts that would be extremely costly to rebuild from scratch and promotes consumer trust, thereby improving participation in trade-in and remanufacturing programs.

Caterpillar, the heavy-equipment company, provides multiple PLE options. Its Cat Reman program offers "same as new" parts and components over time, with an eye to extending the on-site life of each piece of equipment sold. Cat Certified Rebuild is a service whereby customers may return equipment at the end of its serviceable life for restoration to same-as-new condition. On CatUsed.com, customers can buy used equipment from licensed dealers, an excellent example of how a company can prevent high-value products from slipping beyond its reach via the secondary market. On the RPO side, Cat Financial provides various loan and lease options as alternatives to outright ownership. All these business models are supported in part by Caterpillar's ability to monitor the condition of its products remotely, using digital technology and AI, so that it can intervene as necessary—a practice known as installed base management.

Xerox's business model actually encompasses all three basic circularity strategies. Its pay-per-use model both discourages frivolous usage, thereby prolonging the life of the machine, and allows Xerox to retain ownership of its products. The modular design of its copiers' inner workings, most of which are standardized for all models, also furthers PLE. Across product generations, Xerox recycles, reuses, and refurbishes standard components while changing the core imaging technology—thereby keeping machines in action longer. The company complements these approaches with an ambitious material-recycling program (DFR): It claims to be reducing its virgin-resource inputs by hundreds of tons a year, and the internal components of its machines are made from 100% recycled plastics.

Easy to access and easy to process

Products in the lower left quadrant are usually items or components for which a well-oiled recycling infrastructure already exists, as it does for plastic bottles in Norway. Many commodity raw materials also fall into this category. According to the Aluminum Association of the United States, almost 75% of all commercial-variety aluminum ever produced remains in use today. In countries that lack a formal infrastructure for retrieving and returning the metal to manufacturers, enterprising citizens often fill the gap, collecting cans and other discarded aluminum items to exchange for small amounts of cash.

Appropriate circularity strategies for this category will be based on expanding and streamlining processes that already work well. In the United States, Real Alloy, a leading producer of secondary aluminum, is experimenting with minimizing the amount of the metal that is lost to industrial by-products. Norsk Hydro, based in Oslo, one of the largest aluminum companies in the world, is attempting to address the same problem by reducing the quantity of by-products generated in the production process. Incremental DFR innovations like these can make recycling systems even more efficient and profitable for companies.

High-value products that are easy both to access and to process are ideal for circularity, because they require neither a significant business model change nor efforts to facilitate material recovery. This category includes relatively lightweight products whose value lies in their brand rather than in what they're used for or what they're made from. Here there is plenty of scope for companies not already in the circular economy to contemplate entering it.

Patagonia, for example, has parlayed its famed sustainability principles into a used-clothing line for socially conscious consumers. Launched in 2017, the Patagonia Worn Wear initiative invites customers to send in their used Patagonia gear in return for store credit; the clothing is then repaired and resold on the Worn Wear website. Recently Patagonia Worn Wear added a line of hand-sewn clothing called ReCrafted, made from returned items the company considers beyond repair. The approach combines PLE with DFR. At this intersection "same as new" becomes a selling point, allowing Patagonia to tap operational efficiencies while burnishing its brand.

The circularity matrix does not guarantee access to the circular economy. Success or failure with circularity will continue to depend heavily on the receptivity of top leaders, their commitment to sustainable business values, and the willingness of managers at every organizational level to change and adapt. Moreover, your direction will alter as you acquire new capabilities and as new technologies and regulations remove past constraints or impose new ones. But the matrix can help you identify at any one time the strategy best suited to your company's resources, capabilities, and competitive environment.

Originally published in July–August 2021. Reprint R2104D

How to Succeed Quickly in a New Role

by Rob Cross, Greg Pryor, and David Sylvester

A ROLE TRANSITION—WHETHER A PROMOTION, a move to a new organization, or a fresh challenge in your existing job—can be a huge boost to your career and a chance for you to blossom and thrive. You know the drill heading in: Apply your experience and talents to the position, make sure you are accepted by the hierarchy (including your own direct reports), and clinch a few big wins in the first couple of months to demonstrate what you can do.

But in today's hyper-collaborative and dynamic workplaces, successful moves aren't as easy as they once were, even for the most qualified and hardworking people. Too often, transitioning managers and employees don't live up to their organizations' expectations. Gartner surveys indicate that a full 49% of people promoted within their own companies are underperforming up to 18 months after those moves, and McKinsey reports that 27% to 46% of executives who transition are regarded as failures or disappointments two years later. They have the right skills and experience. They understand the company's goals. They've been vetted for cultural fit. So why didn't they quickly excel in their new roles?

We analyzed employee relationships and communication patterns across more than 100 diverse companies and interviewed 160 executives in 20 of them. Our research points to one overlooked prerequisite for transition success: the effective use of internal networks. The people who are the most productive, innovative, and engaged in new roles—the "fast movers"—are those who establish extremely broad, mutually beneficial, uplifting connections from the start. Specifically, they surge rapidly into a broad network; generate pull; identify how they add value, where they fall short, and who can fill the gaps; create scale; and shape their networks for maximum thriving.

In most cases, individual managers must do these things on their own. Only 43% of people surveyed in 2021 by the Institute for Corporate Productivity (i4cp) said their organizations ensured that transitioning employees were onboarded with guidance and support. Only about a quarter said their employers encouraged transitioners to build connections early or create networks to address skills gaps. That should not be the case. Organizations and team leaders can help people in new roles work through the five strategies as part of a well-designed program.

In this article we'll explain why successful transitions are so important to both career and company success, describe how rising demands for collaboration have made networks increasingly critical, and give some advice on implementing each of the fast-mover practices.

Many Transitions + Poor Onboarding = Big Problems

In today's organizations, transitions occur all the time and take many forms. Managers and employees—Millennials and Gen Zers in particular—change jobs far more often than previous generations ever did. A January 2021 survey of 14,000 consumers in nine countries by the IBM Institute for Business Value found that about 20% of workers voluntarily changed employers in 2020, citing desires for such things as job-location flexibility and more-meaningful work, and more than 25% were looking to make a move in 2021. And a Microsoft study of more than 30,000 people in 31 countries indicated that 40% of them were considering leaving their employers in 2021.

Internal moves are increasingly common too. For example, research from i4cp shows that 64% of organizations have recently

Idea in Brief

The Problem

People who transition to new roles—within their organizations or in other ones—often have a hard time doing so successfully. Surveys indicate that 27% to 49% of them underperform.

The Research

Analysis of transitioning employees in 100 diverse companies suggests that the ones who get up to speed and excel most quickly are those who know how to use internal networks effectively.

The Strategies

These people follow five "fast mover" practices: They surge rapidly into a broad network; generate pull by energizing new connections; identify how to add value and who can help them fill skills gaps; use the network to expand their impact; and prioritize relationships that enhance their workplace experience.

undergone or are currently undergoing some form of deliberate culture change. To support such efforts, nearly half of those companies moved leaders at all levels around or out of the organization. According to Gartner, one in three leaders is in transition at any point in time.

Although many companies tout their onboarding processes, it's not clear that those methods are working. In another i4cp survey, only 44% of respondents said their organizations' efforts to onboard external hires achieved desired outcomes, and 88% said that onboarding programs weren't offered to employees who'd been promoted or transferred into new jobs.

Gallup research shows that the cost of replacing an employee is typically one-half to two times that person's salary, depending on seniority and the sophistication of his or her skills. At prepandemic (2017) turnover rates, that translates to nearly $1 trillion a year for U.S. businesses. And that picture may be comparatively rosy, for a few reasons. First, surveys indicate that as workers seek new opportunities and more flexibility post-Covid, voluntary turnover is likely to rise. Second, Gallup's calculations don't factor in the very real network effect of departures. For example, the company suggests that a hypothetical 100-person organization paying an average salary of $50,000 might face staff-replacement costs of $660,000 to $2.6 million a year. But at the Connected Commons—an intentional network dedicated to enabling individuals and organizations to thrive—we've found that the fallout from failed transitions goes beyond acquisition and compensation, because when people underperform and leave, it hurts their coworkers' productivity. Our research shows that, on average, most employees are relied upon by five to 12 colleagues. Let's say someone leaves and five teammates are affected, all of whom take a 5% hit to performance for six months (three months to locate a replacement and three months to get the new hire up to speed). That conservative estimate adds another $845,000 for inefficiencies in the network. (A free calculator is available at network-toolkit.com/connectedtalent.)

Even transitioners who don't fail so badly that they must leave create negative, often unseen ripple effects. According to Gartner, the direct reports of a struggling transitioning leader perform, on average, 15% worse than people who report to a high-performing manager, and they are 20% likelier to leave the organization or be disengaged. The productivity of peers, too, suffers if their work depends on the transitioning employee.

The Hyper-Collaborative Environment

Just as important as the frequency and impact of transitions is what's going on in day-to-day work. More and more companies have identified collaboration across disciplines and units as a way to meet the new business goal of ever-greater agility.

In a 2017 Gartner survey, 67% of organizations indicated that they were using collaborative business models to focus on digital transformation and ranked collaboration as the second-most-important workforce skill, after innovation. Other Gartner research shows that work interdependence is very high. In one study, 82% of organizations reported that their employees must work closely with colleagues to achieve their objectives. In another, 50% of employees said that in the previous three years they had experienced a greater need to coordinate and collaborate to complete their work. (Only 16% said that such demands had shrunk.)

Our own (pre-pandemic) research showed that collaboration in even the most transactional roles had risen markedly, with most leaders and knowledge workers spending 85% or more of their time in collaborative activities—on the phone, on email, and in meetings. For many kinds of jobs, this figure has since increased by five to eight hours a week as a result of remote working, with collaboration earlier in the morning and later at night as employees struggle to keep up with technologies and always-on expectations.

This environment has changed companies' thinking about what's most valuable in their employees' contributions. Gartner reports that companies now view "network performance"—effectiveness at enhancing and capitalizing on others' performance to improve one's own—as equal in importance to the ability to handle tasks individually. A decade ago the former was seen as one-third as important as the latter. And yet only 20% of companies surveyed by i4cp indicated that helping new hires establish critical organizational networks is an objective of their onboarding process. That needs to change.

The Fast-Mover Strategies

In our collective study and analysis of networks, collaboration, and transitions in organizations, we noticed that 10% to 15% of movers became well-connected in a quarter to a third of the usual time, even if they started with few or no contacts, and were reaping the benefits: rapid productivity, innovation, higher engagement, and lower risk of departure. These fast movers showed that people making transitions today don't have the luxury of allowing their network connections to form serendipitously. To be successful, you (and those who onboard you) must be intentional. Here's how.

Surge rapidly into a broad network
Fast movers act as quickly as possible to discover the informal org chart of key boundary-spanning, energizing opinion leaders who are able and willing to help them get things done.

Consider a manager we'll call Holly, who took on the challenge of improving workforce planning in her global professional-services firm. This was not a formal promotion, but it was an important transition. She saw that she needed to talk to helpful and passionate experts who had been thinking about the topic for a long time and weren't afraid to float unusual ideas. Within six weeks she met with dozens of people across various groups to understand the business environment, how the groups operated, and each person's most pressing concerns. Importantly, she ended every conversation by asking for the names of others with whom she should meet or work.

For example, after convening members of the HR function to discuss current processes, she asked each of them to name one or two people in the business units who were well-connected, were frequently tapped for help, or seemed to make a real impact in meetings. She then met with each of those individuals to hear their perspectives on workforce needs. She quickly began to build a broad network encompassing her group, the larger HR function, and people in other business units, corporate functions, levels, and locations who might have a disproportionately positive or negative impact on her success in implementation. She set out to ensure that their impact was uniformly positive.

Holly understood that her transition success depended on creating connections to and goodwill with not only key stakeholders and customers or clients, the organization's formal leaders, and her own team and direct reports, but also people who might not necessarily be viewed as important, such as the *deputies of formal leaders,* who can help transitioners learn about the leaders' goals, motivations, interests, schedules, and workloads so that it becomes easier to make the most efficient use of their time; *colleagues in functional and support roles,* who can facilitate the transitioner's work; and *peers,* who can be sounding boards and sources of information about opportunities and others' views.

Generate pull
John Hagel III, John Seely Brown, and Lang Davidson addressed "the power of pull" in a 2010 book of that name, describing how

people who attract like-minded colleagues and "shape serendipity" benefit themselves and their organizations. Once you've put yourself out there, as Holly did, you want people to come to you, to offer advice, suggest new ideas, and bring you into new projects and your next role.

We noted that while broadening her network, Holly focused on asking questions and listening to better understand others' thinking, needs, and objectives. She also worked to build real relationships, displaying curiosity about others' professional and personal interests and looking for points of commonality. And she left people feeling good, by making it clear that she recognized their status, value, and contributions and by showing that she cared about what she could do for them as much as what they could do for her.

Holly and other fast movers also understand the value of modesty. When transitioning and meeting new people, many of us are tempted to oversell ourselves—to describe our skills and experiences and immediately explain how we'll add value. But heed the adage: "Show, don't tell."

Consider Meredith, an executive who transitions frequently in her industrial-packaging company because others want her, rather than because she requests a transfer or a promotion. She told us that before relating any experience or sharing how her expertise might be relevant, she asks herself whether it will help the person she's speaking to or just cast herself in a better light. If the latter, she keeps it to herself.

Successful transitioners also adjust their approaches and ideas to mesh with new members of their networks. For example, in one new role, Meredith saw that her colleagues were much more consensus-oriented than she was. So when she wanted to move forward on a plan to begin sourcing paperboard from Brazil, which involved weighing cost, quality, and sustainability concerns, she diligently worked to bring everyone on board, rather than making a unilateral decision or settling for a majority vote.

Of course, the fastest way to generate pull is through mutual wins that benefit new contacts as much as they do you. One of the people with whom Meredith linked up was the company's sustainable development officer, who at first opposed her idea because of the rampant falsification of Forest Stewardship Council certification in Brazil. While acknowledging that reality, Meredith made the case that a newly developed grease-barrier coating on the Brazilian paperboard would eliminate the need for plastic liners for food applications. The SDO saw this as a big win for him, so he reversed his position and supported her plan. Impressed by her knowledge and flexibility, he became a friend and an adviser, frequently coming to her with questions, information, and ideas for new initiatives.

Much transition advice focuses on how people should present their own stories and define themselves in others' eyes. We found that fast movers do it differently: They engage with collaborators to cocreate a joint narrative of success.

Identify how you add value, where you fall short, and who can fill the gaps

Whether your main contribution is your knowledge of a key technology, your ability to inspire people, or other skills and intangibles, you can use traditional connections, such as bosses, direct reports, and internal clients, to help you pinpoint exactly what others are expecting you to bring to the table. One executive we interviewed felt completely out of her depth in a new C-suite role that involved meetings on highly technical issues. "I had no idea what to say," she told us. "I didn't think I'd ever be able to speak in those terms." But the CEO reassured her. She recalls his saying, "The reason I picked you for this role was your ability to build momentum and communicate success. You don't have to know all of this."

He also noted that she would need to rely on her network for help. Transitions invariably create skills gaps like this. Most of us either fail to see them or try to bluff our way through. But fast movers get clarity on their value add and then work to improve in the areas where they're weak or find people whose knowledge and skills fill the gaps—which is often a faster and more effective way to come up to speed.

Consider Gary, a manager in an industrial firm, who was promoted to an executive role for his knowledge of a particular product line. He was a 20-year veteran of the organization who was staying within his area of expertise, and yet he soon realized that he was out of touch with some of the terminology being used in his unit. Instead of pretending to understand, he made a list of 33 terms he'd heard but didn't know and asked his team for help. One phrase in particular—"But is it A and K?" which meant "But is it awesome and kewl [cool]?"—opened his eyes to a new way of thinking about the production line. It was said half in jest, but it reflected very real concerns about the company's ability to make its factories more appealing to young workers.

Create scale

Fast movers can not only quickly integrate into their new roles but also get big things done by harnessing the power of those they know. They tap their networks for both *ideation* and *implementation*—that is, they seek help from innovators across the organization who can offer novel solutions to pressing problems and from influencers who can help execute on, spread, and sell those ideas.

A physician we'll call Calvin, who led a palliative-care group in a teaching hospital, illustrates how ideation within a transitioner's network can help achieve scale. When his hospital was integrated into a larger health care system that had little understanding of his field—the discipline of providing relief rather than aggressive treatment for seriously ill patients—Calvin feared that his group might be disbanded, so he started working to broaden his network in the newly merged organization. One contact led to another, and he was soon connected with doctors from specialties such as oncology and geriatrics, who were intrigued by his work, and with people in the health system's communications department. Those conversations sparked an idea: He could use internal publications, speeches, news-media interviews, and other tools of the PR trade to help more colleagues understand palliative care. Because he'd cultivated his new relationships with deliberation, generating pull just as Holly and Meredith did, those new communications-savvy contacts also helped him with implementation. They enthusiastically took up his cause, lending their time and talents to write press releases, edit his blog posts, set up interviews with media outlets, and coach him on public speaking.

Calvin and the other fast movers we've studied make a point of connecting with four types of influencers to achieve scale: *central connectors*, who have big, informal networks that help them socialize ideas and garner support from specific groups; *boundary spanners*, who have ties across groups and geographies and can bridge silos; *energizers*, who create passion and enthusiasm in their interactions, thereby amplifying ideas and engaging the broader organization; and *resisters*—those contrarians and naysayers whose viewpoints must be taken into consideration early, both to improve the idea and, ideally, to get them on your side.

Working through his network, Calvin not only saved his team but established its members as go-to consultants for doctors throughout the hospital system.

Shape the network to maximize personal and professional well-being

Despite the stress inherent in taking on a new role, and all the networking they're doing, fast movers also manage to prioritize their physical and mental health. They don't allow the breadth of their networks to undermine the quality of their relationships or overwhelm them with too many demands for collaboration. They find people who understand, energize, adapt to, and create mutual wins for them just as they did for others. They rely on people who can fill their skills gaps and free them up for more valuable, meaningful, and scalable work.

A carefully crafted, supportive network shields them from some of the pressures of their new roles. As Jerome, a consumer-products marketing-analytics expert tasked with a new initiative, explains, "If I get stuck on one thing, I have six or seven people I can talk to. . . .If the problem is more cerebral, more strategic, there are other people I reach out to." Another transitioner told us that because he has created a larger circle of people "who know me, who I have shared my story with . . . almost like an advisory board," he knows it's always "OK to pick up the phone and talk to somebody."

Some of your new connections should be role models—contacts who show you a path to better work-life balance. An engineer and project manager we'll call Barry told us that his networking efforts in a new role led him to people whose successful management of career and family gave him the confidence to rethink his own patterns of behavior. "When I see them, it gives me a clear understanding that I can have that too, if I take actions to make it happen," he said. He now leaves work early to avoid a traffic-clogged commute, stays offline on weekends, and serves on the board of a local charter school.

If organizations want to ensure that everyone who transitions has a reasonable shot at becoming a fast mover, leaders must develop a networks-first mindset—an understanding of the prime importance of connections in today's highly mobile workforce and how they really function. Many companies pay lip service to supporting networking for new hires and promoted employees. But then they simply provide social hours, urge involvement in external associations, or assume that the bigger your network, the better. Not so. Some of the most effective fast movers make a point of engaging more intentionally with smaller subsets of super-helpful people.

Organizations can further help transitioners by thoughtfully establishing norms for sharing expertise in meetings, pairing newcomers with veterans, and continuing onboarding programs well into the first year. They can develop leadership training that intentionally cuts across silos, conduct "connections audits" to help employees build their networks, and flag ineffective networking practices. And they can deploy coaches and mentors to spread best practices.

Networking for transition doesn't have to be a do-it-yourself exercise. Employers can lead the way in showing people how to quickly build the connections that will help them thrive.

Originally published in November–December 2021. Reprint R2106C

Accounting for Climate Change

by Robert S. Kaplan and Karthik Ramanna

THE AUGUST 2021 REPORT of the UN's Intergovernmental Panel on Climate Change warns that pollution caused by humans has led to an increase in extreme events such as heat waves, heavy precipitation, droughts, and tropical cyclones. Greenhouse gas (GHG) emissions from global economic activity are at the heart of climate change, with atmospheric CO_2 already 50% above its preindustrialization levels.

Unsurprisingly, corporations face growing pressure—from investors, advocacy groups, politicians, and even business leaders themselves—to reduce GHG emissions from their operations and their supply and distribution chains. The nearly 200 CEOs of the Business Roundtable, representing some of America's largest and best-known companies, have responded by issuing a collective statement on their commitment to "the purpose of a corporation," which includes better environmental performance. This commitment is seemingly backed up by action: About 90% of companies in the S&P 500 now issue some form of environmental, social, and governance (ESG) report, almost always including an estimate of the company's GHG emissions.

But ESG in its current form is more a buzzword than a solution. Each of its three domains presents different measurement opportunities and challenges, a fact not adequately addressed by existing disclosure standards. As a consequence, few ESG reports engage meaningfully with the moral trade-offs within the three domains and with the company's profits. Companies also selectively present metrics that portray themselves in a favorable light, resulting in the widespread perception that ESG reporting is awash in greenwash. Not surprisingly, auditors of these reports often resort to double negatives—"We found no evidence of misreporting in the company's ESG report"—and the reports themselves have had little impact on either corporate actions or external stakeholders.

We propose that companies tackle ESG reporting in a more targeted and auditable way. They should first develop specific and objective metrics for the most important and immediate ESG problems, rather than produce catchall reports that are often made up of inaccurate, unverifiable, and contradictory data. GHG emissions are the ideal starting point for such an approach. They represent the most immediate danger to the planet, and they are among the easiest of ESG items to reliably measure and interpret.

Among the companies that already provide GHG estimates in their reporting, most—including 92% of the *Fortune* 500 in 2016—rely on an approach called the GHG Protocol. Introduced in 2001 and updated several times since, this protocol established a common language for GHG measurement that enabled companies to start their environmental reporting journey. It is the default methodology underlying most ESG disclosure standards. But as we show in the following pages, the protocol has serious conceptual errors: The same emissions are reported multiple times by different companies, while some entities entirely ignore emissions from their supply and distribution chains. Indeed, the poor accountability of ESG reports stems partly from the flaws in the GHG Protocol.

The good news is that the defects in the protocol can be fixed. The solution we present here integrates recent advances in measuring emissions by environmental engineers, the introduction of blockchain technologies to accounting and auditing, and two centuries' worth of progress in financial and cost accounting practices. If implemented, our solution will enable GHG reports to approach the relevance and reliability expected of today's corporate financial reports. What's more, much of what is learned through this process can help companies better measure other

Idea in Brief

The Problem

Climate change is an existential threat to life as we know it, but corporations' progress in reducing greenhouse gas (GHG) emissions remains slow, despite the time and energy companies spend on their ESG reports.

Why It Happens

The GHG Protocol—used by more than 90% of *Fortune* 500 companies for those reports—has numerous

basic accounting problems, resulting in a misleading picture.

The Solution

An alternative, comprehensive system, based on established accounting practices, enables the measurement and transfer of GHG emissions along an entire corporate value chain. The authors explain their *E-liability* system and describe its considerable benefits, for both corporations and society at large.

environmentally damaging outputs—and many socially damaging ones as well.

What's Wrong with the GHG Protocol

The protocol identifies three types of GHG emissions and gives explicit guidance for measuring and reporting them.

Scope 1: Direct emissions from sources that are owned or controlled by a company, such as its production and transportation equipment.

Scope 2: Emissions at facilities that generate electricity bought and consumed by the company.

Scope 3: Emissions from upstream operations in a company's supply chain and from downstream activities by the company's customers and end-use consumers.

Scope 1 emissions are the easiest to measure and the most relevant for companies that directly produce large quantities of GHG: fossil-fuel energy companies; mining, metallurgical, and chemical companies; and large-scale agribusinesses. Most other companies, including those in the services sector, produce only small amounts of Scope 1 emissions.

Scopes 2 and 3 essentially cover all GHG emissions indirectly linked to a company's operations. The GHG Protocol carved Scope 2 emissions out of Scope 3 because they are easily measured and allocated to specific companies. Several hundred companies currently report their Scope 1 and 2 emissions. Scope 3 emissions are the fatal flaw in GHG reporting. The protocol's creators included them to encourage companies to exert influence over emissions that they don't control directly. For example, they could buy from or sell to companies with lower Scope 1 emissions, and collaborate with their suppliers and customers to reduce GHG emissions along their value chains. But the difficulty of tracking emissions from multiple suppliers and customers across multitier value chains makes it virtually impossible for a company to reliably estimate its Scope 3 numbers.

Consider the challenges faced by a manufacturer of car doors. Protocol for Scope 3 reporting requires the company to track all GHG emissions from the processes of its upstream suppliers, including the extraction of metallurgical coal and iron ore; the transport of those minerals to a steel producer; the production of sheet steel from the coal, iron ore, and other inputs; and the transport of that steel to its own production facility. The car-door company must also estimate the GHG impact of downstream activities, including transport of the car door to its customer (the automotive-assembly factory), manufacture of the finished car, transport of the car to a showroom, and operation of the vehicle, for perhaps 15 years, by the end-use consumer.

Estimating all those upstream and downstream emissions—especially for companies with long, complex, and multijurisdictional value chains—introduces high measurement error, opening the door to bias and manipulation. Moreover, the Scope 3 protocol requires each company in a value chain to estimate and report GHG emissions from the same activity, which is not only inefficient but generates the duplication mentioned above—an obvious defect in any accounting system.

Not surprisingly, many ESG-reporting companies ignore Scope 3 measurements entirely. But that limits any meaningful contribution to mitigating total emissions across their supply and distribution chains. It also skews responsibility to those suppliers with high-emitting extraction, production, and distribution processes while absolving their customers and consumers of accountability for using heavily polluting components.

We can fix this problem by examining how cost and financial accountants estimate a company's value added—a fundamental corporate measurement task.

When our car-door manufacturer calculates its value added, it does not estimate all the prices paid by all the organizations across all the stages of its value chain. Rather, each organization records only what it pays for goods and services from its immediate suppliers and what it receives when it sells products to immediate customers.

Let's assume, for simplicity's sake, that all transfers of materials in the manufacturer's value chain are made at cost from stage to stage (eliminating the profit margin in the sale and transfer). In this case, the manufacturer's acquisition costs from its immediate suppliers include the total cost of extracting the original materials (incurred by the mining company) plus all the labor, machining, and indirect costs for the materials as they were handled and processed by the sequence of suppliers until the materials reached the car-door manufacturer. The manufacturer adds its own labor, machining, and indirect costs to the acquisition costs to calculate the total manufacturing cost of the door when sold and transferred to the automotive-assembly company. This process continues down the value chain until the car's eventual purchase by a consumer.

The same idea can be applied to GHG emissions.

Tracking Emissions Across an Entire Value Chain

To illustrate, start with the car-door manufacturer's furthest-removed supplier, a mining company in (let's say) Perth, in western Australia. That company extracts the metallurgical coal and iron ore that eventually find their way into the door. It measures its total Scope 1 emissions during a reporting period using a combination of chemistry and engineering, and then, combining that science with cost accounting, assigns its total emissions to the tons of coal, iron ore, and all other minerals extracted during the period. The latter process is similar to the way it estimates the unit production costs of its outputs in a standard activity-based costing system (more on this below). The calculation produces an estimate of GHG emissions per ton of each type of material produced. Whereas financial accounting would record the monetary cost of producing a ton of material as inventory—an asset on its balance sheet—we label the GHG units emitted per ton of extracted material an *E-liability*, reflecting their environmental cost to society.

When the mining company transfers the coal and iron ore to a shipping company, the shipping company assumes the E-liability from the mining company on its E-accounting books (much the way it assumes production inputs as inventory on its financial-accounting books). If the mining company transfers all the materials it mines in the reporting period to downstream entities like the shipping company, its E-liability account at the end of the period will match what it was at the beginning.

As its ocean barge travels from Perth to, say, Port Talbot, Wales, the shipping company adds to its E-liability account the quantity of GHG produced to power the barge's engines. Using basic cost-accounting methods, it assigns the barge's total E-liability to the materials carried on board. At Port Talbot, if the company transfers 38% of the barge's iron ore and 6% of its coal to a steel producer, it will, on its E-accounting ledger, also transfer the same percentages of their E-liabilities to the steel company, which now "owns" those liabilities.

The steel company produces its own Scope 1 emissions by operating furnaces and rolling mills to produce sheet steel. Through the same accounting process, it allocates its bought and incurred E-liability to each ton of sheet steel produced. When the steel is transferred to a railroad company for transport, each ton carries its share of accumulated E-liability—from the mining company, all transportation so far, and the GHG emissions from the steel-production process.

When, several days later, the steel is processed through the receiving dock of the car-door manufacturing company in, say, Solihull, England, the steel's E-liability—which now includes its per-ton share of the emissions from the railroad company's transport from Port Talbot to Solihull—is transferred to the car-door company. This process continues until the consumer who buys the finished car receives a report card on the quantity of GHG emissions produced throughout its manufacture and transportation.

Some companies may choose to directly eliminate GHG from the atmosphere—for instance, by engaging in carbon capture or reforestation. A company that does so can subtract that amount from its E-liability account, subject to auditing, thus reducing its liability transfers along the distribution chain to, eventually, the end-use consumer.

Measuring and Allocating Emissions

This new accounting system requires two basic steps: (1) Calculate the net E-liabilities the company creates and eliminates each period, adding them to the E-liabilities it acquires and has accumulated, and (2) allocate some or all of the total E-liabilities to the units of output produced by the company during the reporting period. For the first step, environmental engineers can estimate the quantity of GHG emissions from a company's primary-source activities, such as burning hydrocarbons for electricity, heat, and transport; producing metals, cement, glass, and chemicals; agriculture involving livestock emissions and deforestation or reforestation; and waste management.

The second step is identical to activity-based costing (ABC) for assigning overhead and other costs to the multiple products and services produced in a given period. Let's assume that the shipping company transfers only two products from Perth to Port Talbot—coal and iron ore. The company acquires the E-liabilities associated with those products from the mine on a per-ton basis. Since the products are also transferred to the steel mill on a per-ton basis, the

FIGURE 10-1

Allocating E-liabilities to products

This exhibit shows how cost accounting would assign to two finished-goods products the E-liabilities associated with their raw materials and production process. For simplicity, we focus on two finished products and two greenhouse gases (CO_2 and CH_4), but the method can be scaled to multiple products and gases.

❶ The manufacturer's beginning-of-period E-liability includes that of two purchased raw materials (RM1 and RM2), created through the extraction, production, and distribution processes used by upstream suppliers.

❷ The manufacturer's production process converts 7 units of RM1 and 6 units of RM2 into 7 units of finished good A (FGA) and 4 units of finished good B (FGB). This process itself generates 20 tons of carbon dioxide (CO_2) emissions and 25 tons of methane (CH_4) emissions, which include E-liabilities purchased from the manufacturer's electricity supplier and depreciation of E-liabilities associated with capitalized equipment.

❸ The calculations below show how the E-liabilities of inputs RM1 and RM2, plus the E-liabilities from the manufacturer's production process, are transferred to the E-liabilities in CO_2 and CH_4 tons/unit of the two finished goods, FGA and FGB, as a function of input quantities and proportion of production time. As these finished goods are sold to the manufacturer's customers, FGA's and FGB's E-liabilities for CO_2 and CH_4 are subtracted from the manufacturer's E-liability accounts (see the exhibit "The E-liability statement") and added to those of its customers.

Finished Good A

	RM1	RM2	PRODUCTION

CO_2: $(4.4 \times 4 + 1.2 \times 4 + 0.6 \times 20) / 7 = 4.9$

CH_4: $(1.8 \times 4 + 3.5 \times 4 + 0.6 \times 25) / 7 = 5.2$

Finished Good B

CO_2: $(4.4 \times 3 + 1.2 \times 2 + 0.4 \times 20) / 4 = 5.9$

CH_4: $(1.8 \times 3 + 3.5 \times 2 + 0.4 \times 25) / 4 = 5.6$

Manufacturer's accumulated E-liabilities

Tons per unit

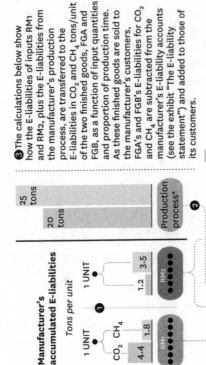

25 tons

20 tons

Production process*

Tons per unit

FGA		FGB
4.9	5.2	5.9	5.6

*Figures shown represent total greenhouse gases produced during production process.

cost accounting is straightforward—the E-liability transfer is analogous to a direct cost in an ABC system.

But as noted, transportation from Perth to Port Talbot generates additional GHG, which must be allocated to the cargo. Iron ore is denser than metallurgical coal, so the E-liabilities associated with transporting the two differ. An ABC-inspired allocation system can apply cost drivers associated with weight, volume, and distance to calculate the precise apportionments.

As with physical inventory, E-liabilities acquired or produced but not transferred to customers in a given period are held for future transfer. This feature of E-liability accounting allows companies to hold and depreciate GHG emissions from fixed assets such as plant and equipment. Consider a steel mill that installs a blast furnace, thus incurring GHG liabilities—such as for emissions from the production and transport of bricks used to line the furnace. These "capitalized" GHG liabilities can be depreciated over each period of the furnace's useful life. In a calculation that replicates cost accounting's allocation of the furnace's acquisition and installation costs to outputs produced during its operation, the E-liability system assigns a proportion of the furnace's E-liability to each period's production.

What Companies Report

With the two accounting steps addressed, companies can report on the stocks and flows of their E-liabilities just as they report on their opening inventory, annual purchases of raw materials, finished goods produced, cost of goods sold, and closing inventory. The equivalent items would be net E-liabilities at the beginning of a period, E-liabilities acquired, net E-liabilities produced during the period, E-liabilities disposed of (sold), and net E-liabilities at the end of the period (see the exhibit "The E-liability statement").

Some environmental activists may fear that transferring a company's entire Scope 1 emissions to downstream customers will enable the company to escape scrutiny for GHG-intensive operations. But just as a good financial analyst looks beneath a company's net income to analyze cost of goods sold and changes in inventory levels, an environmental analyst could interpret the details of a company's purchase, production, and disposal of E-liabilities.

The Benefits of E-Liability Accounting

The E-liability accounting system offers several advantages. Most important, it eliminates the duplicative counting of emissions that is embedded in current Scope 3 measurements. It also reduces

FIGURE 10-2

The E-liability statement

This table shows hypothetical changes to a car-door manufacturer's booked E-liabilities during one accounting period. The opening balance reflects its liability owing to actions in prior periods. Emissions produced by the company from its operations and those transferred to it from its suppliers, including emissions arising from capital investments, are added to the opening balance. Emissions from products purchased by car-assembly plants are then subtracted, and the result is the company's closing E-liability at the end of the period.

E-liability flows	Tons of CO_2
Opening E-liabilities	3,600
Add E-liabilities acquired from suppliers	39,800
Electricity	5,600
Sheet steel	10,600
Glass	5,400
Fabric and plastic	1,200
Other supplies/components	4,800
Capital equipment	12,200
Add E-liabilities directly produced through operations	2,600
Subtract E-liabilities transferred to customers	(32,600)
Closing E-liabilities	13,400
Change in E-liabilities during period	9,800

incentives for gaming and manipulation. A company cannot reduce its reported Scope 1 emissions simply by outsourcing production and then, as is currently possible, ignoring its Scope 3 emissions on the grounds of high measurement error and lack of access to distant suppliers and customers. In the E-liability system, any GHG emissions produced by an outsourced supplier will be transferred to the company upon purchase. What's more, a company can't benefit from understating the E-liability transferred to its customers, because its own end-of-period net E-liability would steadily escalate, suggesting that the company's products are more heavily polluting than customers will accept. Conversely, a company attempting to overstate E-liability transfers to downstream customers would meet with resistance from buyers that preferred to engage with less-polluting suppliers.

The system also allows for its own materiality standard. Currently, several major ESG reporting standards require companies to disclose whenever environmental considerations pose a material *financial* risk to a company. That allows many GHG-intensive processes to go unreported when they have no material impact on a company's financial statements. The E-liability system can apply a materiality threshold specific for GHG, regardless of the financial impact.

Finally, a company's end-of-period E-liability balance can be audited in much the same way that its financial asset and liability accounts are. The external auditors (preferably a team including environmental engineers and cost accountants) can verify the company's internal GHG measurement and allocation models and its purchases and transfers, particularly of GHG-intensive products and services, and reconcile E-liability balances at the beginning and the end of the period. Auditors can cross-check a client's E-liability transactions with corresponding activity in the financial accounts: A red flag would be raised if E-liabilities booked seemed unusually small, relative to industry peers, for the scale of the client's inventory movements in a period.

Blockchain technology, starting with the first stage of production, can be used to accumulate and transfer E-liabilities from stage to stage, reducing accounting and auditing costs across the entire system. Blockchains are especially useful in recording Scope 1 emissions at each stage so that subsequent E-liability transfers must always reconcile with the total Scope 1 number in a value chain. The E-liability system is unlikely to introduce burdensome record-keeping, because it can run on a company's existing financial-reporting and cost-accounting infrastructure, simply using a different unit of measurement: the quantity of GHG emissions rather than the amount of cash and cash equivalents.

Deploying E-Liability Across the Economy

The pressure to do sustainability reporting has been put primarily on publicly traded companies, by their investors and analysts. But restricting the reporting of GHG emissions to such companies would motivate some to go private (and the private ones to remain so) to avoid environmental measurement and disclosure. Thus all companies should be encouraged to report on their E-liabilities, including large private ones such as Bechtel, Bosch, Cargill, Koch, and Mars and those financed through joint ventures, limited partnerships, venture capital, or private equity. Only very small companies with negligible quantities of acquired and produced GHG should be exempt from E-liability reporting.

But corporations are not the only traders in GHG emissions. State-owned enterprises and government agencies, including defense, transportation, energy, and health care, produce and consume many tons of emissions, and they too should be expected to adopt E-liability reporting.

Reliable GHG reporting would also help banks and investment funds respond to demands that they report the emissions of their portfolio companies. Standard-setters such as the Financial Stability Board's Task Force on Climate-Related Financial Disclosures have created formulas for determining how to weight various investment assets on the basis of features such as the nature of the security (debt versus equity, for example) and the degree of control exercised by the investment vehicle over that security. But although those formulas can be useful, the current measurement of the underlying pollutants—the sum of a company's Scope 1, 2, and 3 emissions—remains fundamentally flawed, for the reasons we have described. The E-liability system provides a more reliable way of calculating the total pollution from assets under management as a weighted total of the portfolio companies' end-of-period E-liabilities. Banks and investment funds using the system would have a far better foundation for influencing and reporting on their portfolio companies' environmental impact.

The E-liability approach to GHG accounting would obviate the simplistic labeling of certain sectors, such as fossil fuels and mining, as "sin" industries from which ethical investors should divest. That practice is unlikely to contribute to reducing global emissions, because those industries would not exist at their scale were their outputs not used by "clean" (low Scope 1) companies for their own production and consumption. Our proposed approach recognizes the integrated nature of pollution activities across the economy and encourages all businesses, regardless of sector, to take GHG emissions into account in their product design, purchasing, and selling decisions.

While waiting for new reporting regulation on E-liabilities, large companies—especially signatories to the Business Roundtable's corporate-purpose statement—can put their rhetoric into practice by voluntarily adopting this system and requiring their large suppliers and customers to do the same. That could create competitive advantage by signaling to environmentally sensitive consumers and investors that the company is making auditable progress in reducing total-value-chain GHG emissions. The power of demand- and supply-side markets and competition, informed by E-liability reporting, could encourage corporations to engage in verifiable climate-change action rather than simply issue greenwashed ESG statements.

If governments judged that competitive forces unleashed by robust environmental disclosures were insufficient to achieve targeted reductions in global GHG emissions, the E-liability system would provide them with the tracks on which a variety of carbon-based tax trains could run. They could assess a VAT-like tax on the difference between a company's E-liability transfers and its acquisitions. Companies attempting to avoid the tax by outsourcing the production of heavily polluting products would most likely encounter higher purchase prices to compensate suppliers for the higher taxes being levied on them. Governments could also assess a capital-gains-like tax on large buildups in a company's end-of-period E-liability balance caused by customers' unwillingness to buy the products of heavily polluting production processes. A third option would be to tax the total E-liability of consumers' purchased products and services to raise their environmental sensitivity even further. (Per capita carbon-tax dividends would mitigate the burden on low-income consumers.)

Carbon taxes are not without problems, however. A tax not imposed and enforced globally could engender a flight of corporate activity to nontaxing countries. Offsetting noncompliance with pollution tariffs would be difficult to implement given current international trade laws. And a worldwide carbon tax seems a distant goal in light of geopolitical considerations and issues with enforceability—such as avoidance by state-owned enterprises, especially in countries with less-than-transparent legal systems that already subvert global agreements with hidden subsidies for domestic employers. Driving market-based corporate action on climate change through E-liability reporting may be the fastest way to start systemically reducing GHG emissions.

Going Beyond E

Insights from the widespread deployment of E-liability accounting could inform standards for broader ESG reporting. Of course, no single reporting solution will be relevant for all components of ESG: As noted, ESG is not a single concept. From a reporting perspective, the only thing that E, S, and G have in common is that none is a financial metric. And developing a reporting, evaluation, and investment system for metrics united only by what they are not is hardly a recipe for success.

The lack of a common framework for the three elements leads to contradictions even within a single ESG report. Consider a company under pressure from stakeholders to reduce GHG emitted from its fleet of fossil-fueled vehicles. The company may switch to electric vehicles, resulting in a lower carbon footprint. But what if the battery suppliers for the electric vehicles use conflict raw materials—tin, tantalum, tungsten, and gold (3TG)—mined by indentured prisoners? Or consider a company that has been criticized and excluded from investment portfolios because its ESG report indicates a high rate of workplace accidents. The company may solve its problem by introducing automation and outsourcing, with the result that its report the following year shows many fewer accidents. But what about the unmeasured and unreported loss of employment among former workers and the economic impact on local communities and suppliers?

Some advocates for ESG reporting want to go beyond disclosure to estimate the monetary value of components for inclusion in the company's income statement. Such a statement, they argue, would represent a more comprehensive measure of the true profits of a company. But it is far harder to calculate the value of many ESG components—the impact of a company's labor practices, workforce diversity, and governance, for example—than it is to estimate the accruals based on future cash flows that underlie basic financial reporting.

Consider the decades-long efforts of some accountants just to put human resources on a company's balance sheet, in an attempt to quantify a CEO's statement that "employees are our most valuable asset." Those efforts failed because the measures of employee value were either irrelevant (such as how much was spent historically on hiring and training employees) or they were subjective and unverifiable. Moreover, it would be even harder, if not impossible, to find a formula to *aggregate* the value of ESG's diverse components: Doing so would require some universally accepted ethical code for navigating the intra-ESG trade-offs alluded to above. By treating diverse nonfinancial performance as a single concept, ESG advocates have arguably inhibited fundamental and rigorous thinking about how best to measure and disclose each of ESG's distinctive components.

So how can we move forward on ESG reporting? We propose to start with a few important dimensions on which we can agree about what are "good" and "bad" outcomes and that we can already measure well. Of ESG's three components, *environmental* is the most amenable to rigorous corporate reporting, because it involves objective, physical measurements of the amounts of gases, solids, and liquids that companies use and produce. This is good news, because the easiest component to measure presents the most urgent threat to humanity.

Measuring a company's *social* impact is also amenable to the approach outlined here, but reporting it presents a far greater challenge, because opinions regarding desirable and undesirable corporate behavior differ widely. As with GHG emissions, we can start with those aspects of adverse social performance that almost everyone agrees should be reduced or eliminated: unsafe working conditions, child and slave labor, and bribery and corruption, for example. Despite nearly universal condemnation of those practices, many companies still implicitly accept them in their global supply chains. An S-liability reporting system that captured their incidence in value chains could motivate companies and consumers to be more proactive in eliminating them.

The *governance* component of ESG is the most problematic of the three. Governance is a process, not an outcome. Good governance is valuable only if it leads to better financial, environmental, or societal outcomes. Until good-governance advocates produce valid metrics for outcomes, we believe that companies should treat governance as they now treat internal controls under Sarbanes-Oxley, with qualitative disclosure and external audits of a company's compliance with statutory standards.

———————

In focusing on GHG measurement, we do not deny the relevance of other environmental degradations of soil, water, and biological diversity. Nor do we seek to downplay the benefits of improving companies' societal outcomes and governance practices. But we advocate focusing on what we can and must do well now: improve the measurement and reporting of GHG emissions in an integrated, comprehensive, and auditable way. And in time, the lessons from applying our approach can serve as a model for measuring and tracking other environmental and social outcomes arising from business operations.

Originally published in November–December 2021. Reprint R2106J

Persuading the Unpersuadable

by Adam Grant

THE LEGEND OF STEVE JOBS is that he transformed our lives with the strength of his convictions. The key to his greatness, the story goes, was his ability to bend the world to his vision. The reality is that much of Apple's success came from his team's pushing him to rethink his positions. If Jobs hadn't surrounded himself with people who knew how to change his mind, he might not have changed the world.

For years Jobs insisted he would never make a phone. After his team finally persuaded him to reconsider, he banned outside apps; it took another year to get him to reverse that stance. Within nine months the App Store had a billion downloads, and a decade later the iPhone had generated more than $1 trillion in revenue.

Almost every leader has studied the genius of Jobs, but surprisingly few have studied the genius of those who managed to influence him. As an organizational psychologist, I've spent time with a number of people who succeeded in motivating him to think again, and I've analyzed the science behind their techniques. The bad news is that plenty of leaders are so sure of themselves that they reject worthy opinions and ideas from others and refuse to abandon their own bad ones. The good news is that it is possible to get even the most overconfident, stubborn, narcissistic, and disagreeable people to open their minds.

A growing body of evidence shows that personality traits aren't necessarily consistent from one situation to the next. Think of the dominant manager who is occasionally submissive, the hyper-competitive colleague who sporadically becomes cooperative, or the chronic procrastinator who finishes some projects early. Every leader has an *if . . . then* profile: a pattern of responding to particular scenarios in certain ways. If the dominant manager is interacting with a superior . . . then she becomes submissive. If the competitive colleague is dealing with an important client . . . then he shifts into cooperative mode. If the procrastinator has a crucial deadline coming up . . . then she gets her act together.

Computer code is a string of if . . . then commands. Humans are a lot messier, but we too have predictable if . . . then responses. Even the most rigid people flex at times, and even the most open-minded have moments when they shut down. So if you want to reason with people who seem unreasonable, pay attention to instances when they—or others like them—change their minds. Here are some approaches that can help you encourage a know-it-all to recognize when there's something to be learned, a stubborn colleague to make a U-turn, a narcissist to show humility, and a disagreeable boss to agree with you.

Ask a Know-It-All to Explain How Things Work

The first barrier to changing someone's view is arrogance. We've all encountered leaders who are overconfident: They don't know what they don't know. If you call out their ignorance directly, they may get defensive. A better approach is to let them recognize the gaps in their own understanding.

In a series of experiments, psychologists asked Yale students to rate their knowledge of how everyday objects, such as televisions and toilets, work. The students were supremely confident in their knowledge—until they were asked to write out their explanations step-by-step. As they struggled to articulate how a TV transmits a picture and a toilet flushes, their overconfidence melted away. They suddenly realized how little they understood.

Trying to explain something complex can be a humbling experience—even for someone like Steve Jobs.

A few years ago I met Wendell Weeks, the CEO of Corning, which makes the glass for the iPhone. That relationship began when Jobs reached out to him, frustrated that the plastic face of the iPhone prototype kept getting scratched. Jobs wanted strong glass to cover the display, but his team at Apple had sampled some of Corning's glass and found it too fragile. Weeks explained that he could think of three ways to develop something better. "I don't know that I'd make the glass for you," he told Jobs, "but I'd be very happy to talk with any members of your team who are technical enough to talk this thing through." Jobs responded, *"I'm* technical enough!"

When Weeks flew out to Cupertino, Jobs tried to tell him how to make the glass. Instead of arguing, Weeks let him explain the way his preferred method would work. As Jobs started talking, it became clear to both of them that he didn't fully understand how to design glass that wouldn't shatter. That was the opening Weeks needed. He walked to a whiteboard and said, "Let me teach you some science, and then we can have a great conversation." Jobs agreed, and Weeks eventually sketched out the glass composition, complete with molecules and sodium and potassium ion exchanges. They ended up doing it Weeks's way. The day the iPhone launched, Weeks received a message from Jobs that's now framed in his office: "We couldn't have done it without you."

Let a Stubborn Person Seize the Reins

A second obstacle to changing people's opinions is stubbornness. Intractable people see consistency and certainty as virtues. Once made up, their minds seem to be set in stone. But their views become more pliable if you hand them a chisel.

In a classic experiment, psychologists surveyed students regarding their beliefs about control: Did they see their successes and failures as determined primarily by internal forces, such as effort and choice, or by external forces, such as luck and fate? Stubborn people tend to believe in internal control: They think outcomes can be subject to their will. Next the students evaluated a proposed change to their university's grading system. One-third read a lightly persuasive argument that the new system had been widely accepted at other schools and appeared to be one of the best ever used. Another third read a more forceful argument: This was such a good procedure that they would have to rate it highly. The final third got no persuasive argument. All the students then rated the new proposal on a scale from 1 (very poor) to 10 (very good).

Their reactions depended on their beliefs about control. In people who favored external control, both the light and the forceful arguments generated enthusiasm about the new system. They were comfortable changing their minds in the face of outside influence. People who favored internal control were unmoved by the light argument and were moved in the other direction by the forceful argument. In other words, when someone tried hard to alter their thinking, they snapped back like a rubber band.

A solution to this problem comes from a study of Hollywood screenwriters. Those who pitched fully formed concepts to executives right out of the gate struggled to get their ideas accepted. Successful screenwriters, by contrast, understood that Hollywood executives like to shape stories. Those writers treated the pitch more like a game of catch, tossing an idea over to the suits, who would build on it and throw it back.

Not long ago I was introduced to a former Apple engineer named Mike Bell, who knew how to play catch with Steve Jobs. In the late 1990s Bell was listening to music on his Mac computer and getting annoyed at the thought of lugging the device with him from room to room. When he suggested building a separate box to stream audio, Jobs laughed at him. When Bell recommended streaming video, too, Jobs fired back, "Who the f--- would ever want to stream video?"

Bell told me that when evaluating other people's ideas, Jobs often pushed back to assert his control. But when Jobs was the one generating ideas, he was more open to considering alternatives. Bell learned to plant the seeds of a new concept, hoping that Jobs would warm to it and give it some sunlight.

Research shows that asking questions instead of giving answers can overcome people's defensiveness. You're not telling your boss what to think or do; you're giving her some control over the conversation and inviting her to share her thoughts. Questions like "What if?" and "Could we?" spark creativity by making people curious about what's possible.

One day Bell casually mentioned that since no one would have a Mac in every room, streaming on other devices was going to be a big deal. Then, instead of pressing his argument, he asked, "What if we built a box that would let you play content?" Jobs was still skeptical, but as he imagined the possibilities, he started to take some ownership of the idea and eventually gave Bell the green light. "I knew I'd succeeded when he was arguing my point and proposing the project I'd pitched him," Bell recalls. "By the end he was telling people to get out of my way." That project helped pave the way for Apple TV.

Find the Right Way to Praise a Narcissist

A third hurdle in the way of changing minds is narcissism. Narcissistic leaders believe they're superior and special, and they don't take kindly to being told they're wrong. But with careful framing, you can coax them toward acknowledging that they're flawed and fallible.

It's often said that bullies and narcissists have low self-esteem. But research paints a different picture: Narcissists actually have high but *unstable* self-esteem. They crave status and approval and become hostile when their fragile egos are threatened—when they're insulted, rejected, or shamed. By appealing to their desire to be admired, you can counteract their knee-jerk tendency to reject a difference of opinion as criticism. Indeed, studies in both the United States and China have shown that narcissistic leaders are capable of demonstrating humility: They can believe they're gifted while acknowledging their imperfections. To nudge them in that direction, affirm your respect for them.

In 1997, not long after returning to Apple as CEO, Jobs was discussing a new suite of technology at the company's global developer conference. During the audience Q&A, one man harshly criticized the software and Jobs himself. "It's sad and clear that on several counts you've discussed, you don't know what you're talking about," he said. (Ouch.)

You might assume that Jobs went on the attack, got defensive, or maybe even threw the man out of the room. Instead he showed humility: "One of the hardest things when you're trying to effect change is that people like this gentleman are right in some areas," he exclaimed, adding: "I readily admit there are many things in life that I don't have the faintest idea what I'm talking about. So I apologize for that. . . . We'll find the mistakes; we'll fix them." The crowd erupted into applause.

How did the critic elicit such a calm reaction? He kicked his comments off with a compliment: "Mr. Jobs, you're a bright and influential man." As the audience laughed, Jobs replied, "Here it comes."

As this story shows, a dash of acclaim can be a powerful antidote to a narcissist's insecurity. Not all displays of respect are equally effective, though. It doesn't help to bury criticism between two compliments: The feedback sandwich doesn't taste as good as it looks. Beginnings and ends are more likely to stick in our memories than middles, and narcissists are especially likely to ignore the criticism altogether.

The key is to praise people in an area different from the one in which you hope to change their minds. If you're trying to get a narcissistic leader to rethink a bad choice, it's a mistake to say you admire her decision-making skills; you're better off commending her creativity. We all have multiple identities, and when we feel secure about one of our strengths, we become more open to accepting our shortcomings elsewhere. Psychologists find that narcissists are less aggressive—and less selfish—after being reminded that they're athletic or funny.

The audience member at the Apple developer conference seemed to have an intuitive appreciation of Jobs's narcissistic if . . . then profile. By commending his intelligence and importance, he made it comfortable for Jobs to acknowledge that he didn't know everything about software.

Disagree with the Disagreeable

A final impediment to persuasion is disagreeableness, a trait often expressed through argumentativeness. Disagreeable people are determined to crush the competition, and when you urge them to reevaluate their strategy, that's what you become. However, if you're willing to stand up to them rather than back down, you can sometimes gain the upper hand.

Because disagreeable people are energized by conflict, they don't always want you to bend to their will right away; they're eager to duke it out. When researchers studied how CEOs decided which executives to nominate for board seats at other companies, it turned out that candidates who had a habit of arguing before agreeing with their bosses were more likely to get the nod. It showed that they weren't yes-men or yes-women but were willing to fight for their ideas and change their own minds. In the 1980s at Apple, the leaders of the Mac team gave an award to one person a year who had the temerity to challenge Steve Jobs. Eventually Jobs promoted each winner to run a key division of the company.

In a recent study of ideas pitched by junior people on a health care team, the vast majority were initially rejected by senior leaders. The 24% that made it to implementation did so because their proponents kept fighting for them by refining and repeating pitches, acknowledging and addressing weaknesses, offering proof of concept, and enlisting supporters.

When Apple's engineers brought up the idea of making a phone, Jobs compiled a list of reasons why it wouldn't work. One was that smartphones were for the "pocket-protector crowd." His engineers agreed but then challenged him: If Apple made a phone, how beautiful and elegant could it be? They also tapped the competitive energy he felt toward Microsoft. Wouldn't there be a Windows phone eventually? Jobs was intrigued but he still wasn't sold. Tony Fadell, the inventor of the iPod and a cocreator of the iPhone, told me that people "had to work as a group, not simply in one meeting but possibly over weeks, to get him to change his mind or to see things from another angle." In the case of the iPhone, this argument continued for many months. Fadell and his engineers chipped away at the resistance by building early prototypes in secret, showing Jobs demos, and refining their designs.

Eventually, one big objection remained: The cell phone carriers controlled the networks, and they would force Apple to make a subpar product. Again the team appealed to Jobs's disagreeable tendencies: Could he get the carriers to do it his way? "If we had a powerful enough device," Fadell said, "he could get them to sign up to all of these terms that would remove all of those obstacles." Jobs saw the potential and ran with the idea, winning that battle. "Steve totally reset the relationship with the carriers," former Palm CEO and Handspring cofounder Donna Dubinsky told me. "I always felt that this was his biggest accomplishment."

In 1985, after presiding over product launches that were technical wonders but sales busts, Steve Jobs was forced out of his own company. In 2005 he said, "It was awful-tasting medicine, but I guess the patient needed it." He learned that no matter how powerful his vision was, there were still times when he had to rethink his convictions. When he returned as CEO, it was not only with newfound openness but also with greater determination to hire people ready to challenge him and help him overcome his own worst instincts. That set the stage for Apple's resurgence.

Organizations need strong, visionary executives like Jobs. But they also need employees like Tony Fadell and Mike Bell, suppliers like Wendell Weeks, and stakeholders like the audience member who stood up to complain at Apple's developer conference—people who know how to effectively counteract bosses and colleagues who tend toward overconfidence, stubbornness, narcissism, or disagreeableness. In a turbulent world, success depends not just on cognitive horsepower but also on cognitive flexibility. When leaders lack the wisdom to question their convictions, followers need the courage to persuade them to change their minds.

Originally published March–April 2021. Reprint R2102L

EVA ASCARZA is the Jakurski Family Associate Professor of Business Administration at Harvard Business School.

ATALAY ATASU is a professor of technology and operations management and the Bianca and James Pitt Chair in Environmental Sustainability at INSEAD.

MAUREEN BURNS is a senior partner in Bain & Company's Boston office.

KATHERINE COFFMAN is an associate professor of business administration at Harvard Business School. Her research focuses on how stereotypes affect beliefs and behavior.

ROB CROSS is the Edward A. Madden Professor of Global Leadership at Babson College, founder of the Connected Commons, and the author of *Beyond Collaboration Overload* (Harvard Business Review Press, 2021).

DARCI DARNELL is the head of Bain & Company's customer practice.

CÉLINE DUMAS is a senior manager of operations and sustainability at Accenture France.

PATRICIA GETTINGS is an assistant professor of communication at the State University of New York at Albany. She studies the intersections of personal relationships and organizational commitments and how individuals and organizations negotiate those overlaps.

FRANCESCA GINO is a behavioral scientist and the Tandon Family Professor of Business Administration at Harvard Business School. She is the author of the books *Rebel Talent: Why It Pays to Break the Rules at Work and in Life* and *Sidetracked: Why Our Decisions Get Derailed and How We Can Stick to the Plan.*

ADAM GRANT is an organizational psychologist at Wharton and the author of *Think Again: The Power of Knowing What You Don't Know.*

MARK J. GREEVEN is a Chinese-speaking Dutch professor of innovation and strategy at IMD Business School and a coauthor of *Pioneers, Hidden Champions, Changemakers, and Underdogs.*

BRUCE G. S. HARDIE is a professor of marketing at London Business School.

LINDA A. HILL is the Wallace Brett Donham Professor of Business Administration at Harvard Business School. She is the author of *Becoming a Manager* (Harvard Business Review Press, 2003) and a coauthor of *Being the Boss* (Harvard Business Review Press, 2011) and *Collective Genius* (Harvard Business Review Press, 2014).

ROBERT S. KAPLAN is a senior fellow and the Marvin Bower Professor of Leadership Development, Emeritus, at Harvard Business School. His most recent HBR articles include: "Inclusive Growth: Profitable Strategies for Tackling Poverty and Inequality" (with George Serafeim and Eduardo Tugendhat), "How to Pay for Health Care: The Case for Bundled Payments" (with Michael E. Porter), and "How to Solve the Cost Crisis in Health Care" (with Michael E. Porter).

ELLEN ERNST KOSSEK is the Basil S. Turner Distinguished Professor of Management at Purdue University and formerly was president of the Work and Family Researchers Network. She studies how leaders' support of work-life boundaries, flexibility, and remote work affects women's inclusion and career equality.

KAUMUDI MISRA is an associate professor of management at California State University, East Bay. She studies the role of work-life flexibility practices as a strategic human resource lever for individual and organizational productivity.

FELIX OBERHOLZER-GEE is the Andreas Andresen Professor of Business Administration at Harvard Business School.

GREG PRYOR is a senior vice president and the people and performance evangelist at Workday.

KARTHIK RAMANNA is a professor of business and public policy at Oxford University's Blavatnik School of Government. His HBR articles include "Businesses Must Reclaim Prudent Accounting Principles" and "When the Crowd Fights Corruption" (with Paul M. Healy).

FRED REICHHELD is a fellow at Bain & Company, creator of the Net Promoter System®, and the bestselling author of several books on customer and employee loyalty, including *The Ultimate Question 2.0: How Net Promoter Companies Thrive in a Customer-Driven World*, with Rob Markey.

MICHAEL ROSS is a cofounder of DynamicAction, which provides cloud-based data analytics to retail companies, and an executive fellow at London Business School.

TARAN SWAN is a managing partner at Paradox Strategies, a provider and creator of advisory services, experiences, and tools that enable organizations to navigate the paradoxes of leadership, innovation, and diversity.

DAVID SYLVESTER is the director of executive recruiting and onboarding for Amazon Web Services.

EMILY TEDARDS is a research associate at Harvard Business School.

LUK N. VAN WASSENHOVE is the Henry Ford Chaired Professor of Manufacturing, Emeritus, at INSEAD and leads its Humanitarian Research Group and its Sustainable Operations Initiative.

KATHERINE XIN is the Bayer Chair in Leadership at the China Europe International Business School (CEIBS), in Shanghai.

GEORGE S. YIP is the former vice president of research and innovation at Capgemini Consulting; an emeritus professor at Imperial College Business School, in London; and a visiting professor at Northeastern University, in Boston.

Index

accommodation, in flexible work,
4–5
accountability
for decisions, 60–61
for unconscious bias, 79
activity-based costing (ABC),
153–154
Adidas, 124, 129
aggregation, marketing AI and,
85–86, 91–92
agile methodology
in decision-making, 54–55
killing "walking zombies" and,
64–65
AI
marketing, 83–92
sales interfaces enabled by,
114–115
Alibaba, 108, 109–110, 113, 114
alignment
around purpose for
decision-making, 63–66
circular business model and, 122
marketing AI and, 84, 90–91
Alipay, 15, 109–110, 114
Aluminum Association, 131–132
Amazon, 43, 44, 47
on assembly processes, 103
product recommendations, 111
Twitch and, 113
Anderson, Ray, 121–122
Ant Group, 108
Apple, 46, 47
design for recycling at, 129–130
Jobs and, 165, 167, 168, 169–170,
171–172
arrogance, 166–167
Ascarza, Eva, 83–92
Asgari, Shaki, 74
assumptions, examining, 73–74,
89–92
asymmetry, marketing AI and, 85, 91
asynchronous media, 25–26

Atasu, Atalay, 121–133
automation, 28–29

Bain, 100, 102
Bank of America, 2
Barra, Mary, 15
BayCare, 42
Bell, Mike, 168
Belouizdad, Zeina, 15
Best Buy, 43–44
BILT, 103–104
BioPak, 130
blockchain technology, 157–158
Bosch Power Tools, 124
Boston Consulting Group, 83
boundaryless working, 4, 5–7
Brown, John Seely, 140–141
burnout, 8
disincentives for using flexibility
and, 14–15
tech exhaustion and, 25
Burns, Maureen, 93–105
business model, circular. See
circular business model
business models, collaborative,
138–139
Business Roundtable, 147, 159
ByteDance, 108

Cainiao, 115–116
California, Proposition 22, 117
California Closets, 101, 102
carbon capture, 153
carbon taxes, 159–160
careers
flexible work and, 3, 5
global "shecession" and, 6–7
how to success quickly in new
roles, 135–145
proximity bias and, 23
Caterpillar, 131

central connectors, 144

CertaPro, 101, 102

chatbots, 114

checklists, for flexible work, 10, 13–14

childcare
value-based strategy and, 45
women's inequal share of, 3, 5, 6–7

China, customer journey in, 107–119
customer loyalty and, 117–119
embedded digital evaluation in, 112–113
entry points in, 109–112
logistics in, 115–116
seamless sales in, 113–115

circular business model, 121–133
circularity matrix and, 124–133
design for recycling strategy for, 124, 127–128, 129–130
feasibility assessment for, 125–132
product life extension strategy for, 124, 130–131
retain product ownership strategy for, 122–123, 127–128, 130–131
strategies for, 122–124

circular economy, 121, 132–133

circularity matrix, 124–133

climate change, accounting for, 147–163
E-liability accounting, 152–160
ESG reporting and, 147–148, 160–162
GHG Protocol for, 148–151
measuring and allocating emissions and, 153–155
tracking emissions across the value chain and, 151–153
what companies report and, 155–156

Clinical Research Pharmacy, 57

Coffman, Katherine, 67–81

cognitive swift trust, 24–25

collaboration
employee transitions and, 138–139
marketing AI and, 86–87

Collective Voices podcast, 74–75

communication
about four-day workweeks, 32–33
about decisions, 60–61
about flexible work, 10, 15–16
good fights and, 62–66
marketing AI and, 86–92
persuasive, 165–172
in unconscious bias training, 75–76

complements, value creation with, 45–46

compromise, 56–57

conflict
avoidance of, 56–57
encouraging good fights and, 62–66

Connected Commons, 138

consultation, for decisions, 60–61

Corning, 74–75, 76, 80, 167

Covid-19 pandemic
cyberattacks in, 27–28
flexible work in, 4, 6–7, 8, ix
job changes and, 137
Pfizer vaccine in, 54, 59, 63, 66, x

Cross, Rob, 135–145

curiosity, 77

customer journey, 107–119

customer lifetime value (CLV), 98

customers
as advocates (See Net Promoter System (NPS))
attracting with value-based strategy, 42
earned new, 99–101
involving in decision-making, 55–57

long-term value of referrals by, 101–103
loyalty of, 104–105, 117–119
power of advocacy of, 94
radical engagement with, 117–118
value creation for, 42–45, 52
willingness to pay of, 38–39, 45
CVS, 117
cybersecurity, hybrid working models and, 27–28

Dada, 114
Darnell, Darci, 93–105
Dasgupta, Nilanjana, 74
data
   focus on for productive debate, 63
   informed decision-making and, 58–59
   privacy rules, 111
   unconscious bias training and, 69, 77–80
   visualization of, 58–59
   on waste and missed opportunities, 89
   on work optimization, 34–35
data science teams, 86–92
Davidson, Lang, 140–141
decision-making, 53–66
   avoiding traps in, 56–57
   clear decision rights and, 60–61
   data-informed, 58–59
   focus on purpose in, 63–66
   good fights in, 62–66
   marketing AI and, 85–86
   unconscious bias and, 80
defensiveness, 168–169
Deloitte, 5–6
Delta Air Lines, 14, 59
denial, of bias, 71–72
design for recycling (DFR) strategy, 124, 127–130

detractors, 93–94
Devine, Patricia, 69–70
DFR (design for recycling) strategy, 124, 127–130
Dianxiaomi, 114
digital red envelopes, 118
disagreeableness, 170–172
discovery-driven learning, 61–62
discrimination, gender-based, 3, 5. *See also* women
diversity and inclusion
   breaking stereotypes and, 74–75
   in decision-making, 55–59
   encouraging interactions among groups and, 76–78
   flexible work and, 8, 17–18
   hybrid work designs and, 21–22
   unconscious bias training and, 67–81
Dobbin, Frank, 67
documentation
   of decision-making processes, 87–88
Domino's, 117
Dong Mingzhu, 112
Douyin, 107–108
DreamBox Learning, 56
DSM-Niaga, 129
Dubinsky, Donna, 172
Dumas, Céline, 121–133

earned growth, 95–104
   calculating, 98–101
   origin of, 95–98
   reporting, 103–104
earned growth rate, 96
earned growth ratio, 96
earned new customers (ENC), 99–101
eBay, 58
Economist, 107

ecosystems, 108, 109–110
Effifuel, 128
Einride, 117
E-liabilities, 152–160
emotional trust, 24–25
empathy, 75–76
employees. *See also* flexibility, at
    work
    attracting with value-based
        strategy, 42
    cost of replacing, 137–138
    gig workers, 116, 117
    how to succeed quickly in new
        roles, 135–145
    intentions of to leave, 19–20
    safe environment for questioning
        by, 33–34
    value creation for, 42–45
    willingness-to-sell wage of, 39–41
empowerment
    decision rights and, 60–61
    for flexible work, 12–14
ENC (earned new customers),
    99–101
energizers, 144
engagement, radical, 117–118
environmental, social, and governance
    (ESG) reporting, 147–149, 160–161
Ericsson, 117
ESG. *See* environmental, social, and
    governance (ESG) reporting
Evergreen Services Agreement
    (ESA), 121–122
Excite, 41–42
external control, 167–169
EY, 77

facial recognition, 15
Fadell, Tony, 171–172
fan marketing, 118
fast-mover strategies, 139–145

feedback
    proximity bias and, 23
    on unconscious bias, 78–79
First Republic Bank, 95–96
FirstService, 101–103
Fish, Kathy, 61–62
flexibility, at work, 1–36
    four-day workweek and, 29–36
    accommodation as, 4–5
    availability of to all employees,
        8–9
    boundaryless working as, 4–7
    disincentives for using, 14–15
    employer biases about, 2–3
    empowering employees for, 12–14
    experimentation with and mea-
        surement of, 16–17
    global workforces and, 17–18
    hybrid work, 18–29
    implementation of, 1–2
    leadership in, 1–2, 8, 14, 15–16
    learning curve with, 18
    managing, 1–2
    predictable schedules for, 39–40
    structures and policies for, 9–12
    synergies from bundling types of,
        10, 11–12
    traditional approaches to, 4–7
    true, 3, 7–18
    types of, 11–12
fluidity, in office spaces, 27
Forest Stewardship Council
    certification, 142
four-day workweek, 29–36
    communicating about, 32–33
    goals and metrics for, 31–32
    piloting, 33–35
    scaling up and reiterating, 35–36

GAAP, 99, 101
Gallup, 137–138

Gap, 39–40
Gartner, 135, 137, 138, 139
GCS (Global Clinical Supply). *See* Global Clinical Supply (GCS)
gender gap, 3, 5, 6–7, 17–18
General Data Protection Regulation, 111
General Motors, 15, 114–115
Gen Z, 136
Geotab, 117
Gettings, Patricia, 1–18
GHG Protocol, 148–151
gig workers, 116, 117
Gino, Francesca, 67–81
Global Clinical Supply (GCS), 53–54, 57, 58–61, 65–66
goals
    four-day workweek and, 31–32
    flexible work and, 8
Google, 15, 42
Gorenje, 125
governance, 162
Grant, Adam, 165–172
Gree Electric, 112
greenhouse gas (GHG) emissions, 147
    E-liability accounting for, 151–160
    ESG reporting on, 147–148
    GHG Protocol for, 148–151
    measuring and allocating, 153–155
    tracking across the value chain, 151–153
    what companies report and, 155–156
Greenwald, Anthony, 74
greenwashing, 148
Greeven, Mark J., 107–119
growth
    earned, 95–104
    managerial focus on, 38–39
    potential for in unconscious bias training, 72–73
Gucci, 38

Hagel III, John, 140–141
Hardie, Bruce G. S., 83–92
Harkins Theatres, 45
health, 8
    shaping networks for, 144–145
    tech exhaustion and, 25
health care. *See also* Pfizer
    disincentives for using time off in, 14
    self-scheduling in, 13
Hema Fresh, 113
Hennick, Jay, 101
Hill, Linda A., 53–66
Hill, Molly, 79–80
hiring, unconscious bias in, 71–72
human augmentation, 29
hybrid working models, 2, 18–29
    adjusting, 20–21
    best approaches to, 19–21
    employee desire for, 18–19
    future of, 28–29
    inclusivity in, 21–22
    office space and, 26–27
    performance measurement and, 24
    remote onboarding and, 22–23
    tech exhaustion and, 25
    transitioning to, 22

i4cp, 137
IBM, 2, 5–6
IBM Institute for Business Value, 136
ideation, 143–144
Ikea, 103
implementation, 143–144
Implicit Association Test, 70
incentive structures, four-day workweeks and, 35
influencers, 112–113, 118
inner circles, expanding, 76–77

innovation
in China, 108
discovery-driven learning and, 61–62
driving with decision-making, 53–66
value drivers and, 50
Instagram, 112
Institute for Corporate Productivity, 136
Interface, 121–122
internal control, 167–169
iPhone, 47, 171–172

JD.com, 108, 110, 113–114
job rotations, 9
Jobs, Steve, 165, 167, 168, 169–172
Joly, Hubert, 44
Jumbo, 15

Kalev, Alexandra, 67
Kaplan, Robert S., 147–163
Kelly, Erin, 67
key opinion leaders (KOLs), 108, 118
Kickstarter, 29–30
Kindle, 45, 47
Kossek, Ellen Ernst, 1–18
Krenek, Meena, 26–27
Ku, Michael, 63, 65–66

labor regulation, 117
leaders
four-day workweek and, 30–31
customer loyalty and, 104–105
in decision-making, 56, 66
flexibility management and, 1–2, 8, 14, 15–16
persuading the unpersuadable, 165–172
psychological safety and, 62–66
lean methodology
in decision-making, 54–55
at P&G, 61–62
learning
discovery-driven, 61–62
unconscious bias training and, 67–81
Lehigh Technologies, 128
Li Bin, 112
LifeWorks, 9–10
Li Jiaqi, 108, 113
Lipstick King, 108, 113
Liu Tao, 112–113
livestreaming, 112–113
Li Xiaolu, 112–113
Lockhart, Charlotte, 29–36
locus of control, 167–169
logistics integrators, 115–117
loyalty programs, 118, 119
Lydia, 15, 111–112

Ma, Pony, 108
marketing, fan, 118
marketing AI, 83–92
aggregation in, 85–86, 91–92
alignment in, 84, 90–91
asking the right questions for, 84, 90–91
asymmetry in, 85, 91
communication breakdowns and, 86–87
communication framework for, 87–92
leveraging granular predictions in, 85–86, 91–92
marketing problem definition and, 87–88
potential gains from, 92

value of being right *vs.* costs of
   being wrong in, 85, 91
waste and missed opportunities
   and, 88–92
Markey, Rob, 100
materiality standards, 157
McDonald's, 9
McKinsey, 135
media, lean versus rich, 25–26
medium maximizers, 30–31
Meituan, 108, 118
mentors, 78–79
metrics. *See also* Net Promoter
   System (NPS)
   four-day workweek and, 31–32,
     34–35
   for flexible work, 10, 16–17
   for hybrid employees, 24
   medium maximizers and focus
     on, 30–31
   on unconscious bias, 79
   on unconscious bias training, 69
Michelin, 127–128
Microsoft, 16
   on job transitions, 136
   unconscious bias training at, 72,
     73, 80
   Work Trend Index, 18
Miele, 124
Millennials, 2, 136
mindset
   four-day workweek and,
     30–31
   network-first, 145
Misra, Kaumudi, 1–18
modesty, 141
Morneau Shepell, 9–10
mutual wins, 141–142

narcissism, 169–170
Neeley, Tsedal, 18–29

Net Promoter System (NPS), 93–105
   credibility of, 94
   earned growth–based, 95–105
   long-term value of referrals and,
     101–103
   objective of, 93–94
net revenue retention (NRR), 98–101
network performance, 139
networks, internal, 136, 139
   creating scale and, 143–144
   shaping to maximize well-being,
     144–145
Nike, 17, 40, 129
NIO, 112
norms, 32, 36, 145
Northern Trust, 10, 12, 16–17
NPS. *See* Net Promoter System (NPS)
NRR (net revenue retention), 98–101
NTWRK, 113
nudges, 80
Nuro, 117

Oberholzer-Gee, Felix, 37–52
office space, hybrid working models
   and, 26–27
onboarding
   remote, for hybrid work, 22–23
   transitioning employees, 136–145
organizational culture
   disincentives in for using time off,
     14–15
   good fights and, 62–66
Otto Group, 111
overtime, 15

Pager, Devah, 71–72
Parkinson's law, 25
Parley for the Oceans, 124
Patagonia, 124, 132
Patterson, Scott, 101–103

Peacebird, 114
Peloton, 119
PepsiCo Work That Works
    program, 20
performance
  hybrid work and, 22, 24
  network, 139
  transitions and, 136, 138
performance reviews, bias in,
    73–74
Perkins and Will, 26–27
personality, persuasiveness and,
    165–166
perspective, 75
persuading the unpersuadable,
    165–172
  arrogance and, 166–167
  disagreeableness and, 170–172
  narcissism and, 169–170
  subbornness and, 167–169
Pfizer, 53–54, 57, 58–59, 60–61,
    65–66
P&G, 57, 61–63
Picnic, 15
pilots, for four-day workweeks,
    33–35
Pinduoduo, 108, 114
plastic bottle recycling, 125–126
platforms, 110, 113
PLE (product life extension)
    strategy, 124, 130–131
policies
  cybersecurity, 27–28
  for flexibility at work, 9–12
  unconscious bias and,
    80–81
pooling work, 21
praise, 169–170
prejudice habit-breaking,
    69–70
Prescott, Sidney Madison, 29
privacy regulations, 111

problem-solving
  diverse perspectives in, 55
  marketing AI and, 87–88
processes
  adjusting for four-day work-
    weeks, 32–33
  continuous, experimentation
    and, 61–62
product evaluations, 112–113
productivity
  four-day workweek and, 29–36
  flexible work and, 2–3
product life extension (PLE)
    strategy, 124, 130–131
product recommendations, 110–111
profitability
  flexible work and, 6
  strategy initiatives and, 37–38
  value-based strategy and, 41–42
profit pools, 46–47
Progressive, 44–45
promoters, 93
proximity bias, 23
Pryor, Greg, 135–145
psychological safety, 33–34, 62–66
pull, generating, 140–142
purpose
  corporate, climate change and,
    147, 159
  customer loyalty and, 104–105
  in productive debate, 63–66
PwC, 5–6

QR codes, 15
Quest Diagnostics, 44
questions
  good fights and, 62–63
  for marketing AI, 84
  overcoming defensiveness with,
    168–169
Quillian, Lincoln, 71–72

Ramanna, Karthik, 147–163
Real Alloy, 132
recycling, 125–126
    design for, 124, 127–130
reforestation, 153
Reichheld, Fred, 93–105
remote learning, 21–22
Rent the Runway, 123
resisters, 144
responsibility, for decisions,
    60–61
retain product ownership (RPO)
    strategy, 122–123, 127–128,
    130–131
robotic process automation (RPA),
    28–29
role transitions, 135–145
Roosevelt, Theodore, 25
Rooster Teeth, 113
Ross, Michael, 83–92
rotations, work, 21
routing technology, 116
RPA (robotic process automation),
    28–29
RPO (retain product ownership)
    strategy, 122–123, 127–128

sales channels, 113–114
scale, creating, 143–144
Schmidt Zeevis, 15
self-scheduling, 13–14
Shein, 119
Shift Messenger, 40
shift-swapping, 13–14
Singles' Day, 114
Sloan Management Review, 83
social impact, measuring, 162
Sony, 45
spill, 88–89
spoil, 88–89
Spotify, 29

stakeholders
    communicating to about four-day
        workweeks, 33
    communicating to about work
        flexibility, 16
    hybrid work guidelines and, 20
Starbucks, 72, 75, 77, 79–81
stereotypes, 74–75
strategic overload, 37–52
strategy
    unconscious bias training, 79–81
    value-based, 38–52
structure, for flexibility at work,
    9–12
stubbornness, 167–169
substitutes *vs.* complements, 45–46
success
    defining for four-day
        workweeks, 32
    marketing AI and, 88–89
    strategy initiatives and, 37–38
Suncor, 73
suppliers, value creation for,
    42–45
supply chains, 121
    reverse, 125–126
sustainability. *See* circular business
    model
Swan, Taran, 53–66
Sylvester, David, 135–145
synchronous media, 25–26

Taobao, 109–110, 113, 118
TaskRabbit, 103
Tata Pravesh, 118
Tatra, 48, 49–50
TD, 118
teams
    charters for, 10, 12
    flexible work and, 10, 12
    trust in hybrid work, 24–25

technology
    blockchain, 157–158
    exhaustion from, 25
    for hybrid workers, 23
    matching with work needs, 25–26
    robotic process automation and,
        28–29
    routing, 116
    value-based strategy and, 46
Tedards, Emily, 53–66
teleworking, pros and cons of, 6–7.
    See also flexibility, at work
Telia, 117
Tencent, 108
tetrads, 60–61
Third Place, 76
TikTok, 107–108, 112, 114
time off, 12, 14
Tmall, 110–111, 118
trade-offs, 52
trust, hybrid work teams and, 24–25
Twitch, 113

Uber, 42
UBS, 17
The Ultimate Question 2.0
    (Reichheld), 94
unconscious bias training, 67–81
    acting on awareness of bias and,
        71–75
    creating empathy and, 75–76
    effective model for, 69–71
    encouraging interactions among
        groups and, 76–78
    failure of conventional, 67
    flaws in conventional, 68–69
    goal of, 67
    good practices and continued
        learning in, 78–79
    impact of effective, 68
    strategy for, 79–81

understaffing, 14
UN Intergovernmental Panel on
    Climate Change, 147
University of Wisconsin, 69–70

value
    extracting from circular
        models, 125
    GHG reporting and, 151
    identifying how you add, 142–143
    recovering from products, 126–132
value-based strategy, 38–52
    in action, 40–47
    elements of, 38–40
    employee benefits of, 39–40
value capture, 46–47
value creation, 46–47
value drivers, 49–51
value maps, 48, 49–52
value sticks, 40, 41
Van Wassenhove, Luk N., 121–133
video livestreaming, 112–113
VIP.com, 110
Viya, 113, 118

Walmart, 43, 115, 117
Warby Parker, 96, 98
Wayfair, 103
Webfleet Solutions, 117
WeChat, 112, 114
WeChat Pay, 15, 110
Weeks, Wendell, 167
Weibo, 112
WhatsApp, 61
Whillans, Ashley, 29–36
willingness to pay (WTP), 38–39, 40,
    41, 45–46, 47, 49
willingness-to-sell (WS) wage,
    39–40, 41, 47, 49
wind turbines, 128

women
  flexible work and, 3, 5, 6–7
  in health care, self-scheduling
     and, 13
  performance review bias and,
     73–74
Woolley-Wilson, Jessie, 56
work, flexibility at, 1–36
work-life balance
  flexible work and, 2, 6–18
  four-day workweek and,
     29–30
  pay equity and, 17–18
WTP. *See* willingness to
     pay (WTP)

Xerox, 123, 131
Xiaohongshu (RED), 110
Xiaomi, 118
Xin, Katherine, 107–119

Yip, George S., 107–119
Ymatou, 110
Yonghui, 114

Zalando, 111
Zara, 44, 119
Zhihu, 113
Zhishi Xingqiu, 113

Engage with HBR content the way you want, on any device.

With HBR's subscription plans, you can access world-renowned case studies from Harvard Business School and receive four **free eBooks**. Download and customize prebuilt **slide decks and graphics** from our **Data & Visuals** collection. With HBR's archive, top 50 best-selling articles, and five new articles every day, HBR is more than just a magazine.

Subscribe Today
HBR.org/success